Is Your Church HEAVENLY?

A Question from Christ for Every Christian

By John Meacham
with
Dr. Lon Ackelson

ZOË LIFE
PUBLISHING
WORDS TO LIVE BY

Published by:
Zoë Life Publishing
P.O. Box 871066
Canton, MI 48187 USA
www.zoelifepub.com

All Scripture quotations, unless otherwise indicated, are taken from the New International Version of the Bible ®. Copyright © 1973, 1978, 1984 by International Bible Society 1977, 1995 by The Lockman Foundation.

Take note that the name satan and associated names are not capitalized. We choose not to give him any preeminence, even to the point of violating grammatical rules.

Author: John Meacham
Cover Designer: John Jorif
Editorial Team: Dr. Lon Ackelson, Lighthouse Editing
                   and Jessica Colvin, Associate Editor

First U.S. Edition 2008

Publisher's Cataloging-In-Publication Data

Meacham, John

Is Your Church Heavenly

Summary: A book of reflective, biblically-sound, Spirit-led teachings for church leaders, members, small groups, and congregations to pick apart and delve into so the suggestions can be utilized to make heavenly changes in their daily Christian walk.

10 Digit ISBN 1-934363-34-0 perfect bound, softcover.
13 Digit ISBN 978-1-934363-34-8 perfect bound softcover

    1. Christian Living   2. Religion   3. End-times

Library of Congress Control Number: 2008933693

For current information about releases by *John Meacham* or other releases from Zoe Life Publishing, visit our web site: *http://www. zoelifepub.com*

Printed in the United States of America
#v2.4 07 23 08

*This book is offered for the Glory of God
and the good of Christ's Church.*

Is Your Church
HEAVENLY?

A Question from Christ for Every Christian

By John Meacham
with
Dr. Lon Ackelson

Contents

Foreword

Every time I read *Is Your Church Heavenly?* I am uplifted, encouraged, edified and convicted. It is so amazing how this book lays such a strong foundation for any believer to build upon—not to be just be a hearer of the Word, but a doer of the Word.

Is Your Church Heavenly? is a book of reflective, biblically-sound, Spirit-led teachings for church leaders, members, small groups, and congregations to pick apart and delve into so the suggestions can be utilized to make heavenly changes in their daily Christian walk. Solomon said in, Ecc 1:9, "What has been will be again, what has been done will be done again; there is nothing new under the sun." This holds true for today. *Is Your Church Heavenly?* pulls Scripture from Revelation and proves how the Lord's instructions are timeless and eternal. It provides an in-depth look into the letters from Christ to the seven churches in need of reform, inviting them to make monumental changes which are still applicable today—in many ways even more so.

The honest truth is, I am sick and tired of Sunday-only Christians. The relationship we have with Christ should be vital, vigorous, and whole-hearted with every breath we take and every word we speak. Our walk should light the path for others to follow. I believe, as Christians, we all desire to practice what we preach. The problem is that *wanting* doesn't get you anywhere…you have to have a game plan in order to reach the goal.

This is where John's book shines. It is the perfect playbook for churches, leaders, and members. The book is more than a Bible study. It is a group of eye-opening, hard to hear lessons. It is honest, sometimes harshly so, yet the honesty is straight from the Holy Spirit and needs to be shared with Christians worldwide.

I believe this book is the clarion call, the early wake-up call so we can get ready before the final horn sounds. It is saying to the church, "Wake up! Have some passion! Catch on fire for Jesus!"

I am so honored and privileged to be a part of bringing this important clarion call to all of God's children throughout the world.

—**Sabrina Adams**
Founder and Director
Zoë Life Publishing

Prologue

While occupying a motel room in Israel the last week of January 2005, I began writing *Is Your Church Heavenly?*. The Lord Jesus Christ led me in completing this book both during my time in Israel and after I returned home. The first seven chapters parallel the seven letters Christ wrote that the Apostle John recorded in the second and third chapters of Revelation and the eighth chapter is a call from Christ for church reform.

My journey to Israel occurred after Jesus appeared to me in three dreams. Each dream was of a special appearance of Christ on earth and they are described in my article, "My Dreams of the Second Coming" in the January 2004 issue of *Christian Literature & Living*. In the first dream, Christ flew down to the earth on a cloud, and this frightened me. In the second dream, Christ told me, "Do not be afraid; I have work for you to do." Then in the third dream, church leaders and I were on a hilltop at the Sea of Galilee watching Jesus descending on a cloud to return to earth.

On Father's Day, 2003, I learned the date of the third dream plus instructions to the exact location in Israel where Jesus might return. God's Spirit let me know that Christ might return to Galilee on January 25, 2005.

On Monday, January 17, 2005, I told Israel's El Al Airline officials that I was going to Galilee as a tourist and would do some writing there. The officials frostily asked me what kind of writing I planned to do, their tone suggesting to me that some writing areas did not meet their approval. After I replied, "*Christian* writing," smiles replaced frowns. I was released to get my baggage and rent a car. Christian travelers are welcome in Israel.

After getting my rental car, I drove to Tiberius. I discovered that Tiberius is the major seaside city on the Sea of Galilee where Jewish people live today. Capernaum, the seaside headquarters for Jesus during His Galilean ministry, is today only a tourist site, as are many other seacoast cities that thrived in New Testament times. I became a guest in a motel right across the street from the commemorative site of Jesus' baptism. After breakfast on Tuesday morning, the eighteenth, I returned to my room to review the directions I received in 2003. Using a map of the area, I then left my motel and set out to find the site for Christ's return a week later.

Led by God's Spirit, I drove from the west coast of the Sea of Galilee to the north coast; then I turned right onto Road Ninety-Two and drove along the northeastern side of the Sea of Galilee. My route from Tiberius had followed the coastline and as I traveled alongside the northeastern shore, I knew that the return site was getting near.

It was the stones.

Large, dark stones lined the northeastern corner of the Sea of Galilee. Some stones were stacked in orderly piles, and other stones were lying around loosely.

The stones were a major departure from what I saw on the west and north shores of the Sea of Galilee. When I saw them, I sensed the power of the Holy Spirit coming upon me. All I could think of was what Jesus said on the first Palm Sunday about the stones crying out if His people did not proclaim that He was the Messiah (Luke 19:40). As I drove and gaped at these stones, I knew I was nearing the site of Jesus' return.

Then, I saw the lights. In my premonition, God's sign for the return site indicated that there would be some type of outside lights on the property. On the left side of the road, spotlights surrounded what looked like a large stage built from earth and stones. This site was indicated on a road sign as DALIYYOT. At nine A.M. on my first day in Israel, I pulled into the parking area to begin the seven-day wait for Christ and to pray for the Church. Though the spiritual leaders I saw in my third dream did not materialize, I still knew that I needed to stay the full week.

My plan for each day was to arrive at nine A.M. and stay until nine nineteen. My daily prayer for the Church was, "Come, Lord Jesus! Come!" I closed with the words from Revelation 22:17, "The Spirit and the Bride say, 'Come! [Lord Jesus! Come!]'" I walked several times around the stage, repeating these words, until nineteen minutes had passed.

In the most vivid dream of Christ's return (my third dream), I had the responsibility to bring church leaders with me to the return site in Israel to meet with Him. I invited a pastor I knew to join me in Israel, but he regretted that he and his wife had another engagement for the same period. My article, "My Dreams of the Second Coming" in *Christian Literature & Living* in the January 2004 issue, closed with an invitation for Christian readers to join me in Israel a year later— but none of the readers responded. Although I was not able to carry out the task of my third dream, at least I was here and, even by myself, I could pray and wait. My Father's Day experience that conveyed all the details that led me to Daliyyot filled me with great expectations.

For the next seven mornings (excluding Sunday when I attended the morning worship service at the Church of the Multiplication of the Loaves and Fishes), I returned to Daliyyot and prayed for Christ to return and reform His Church.

After each daily prayer at the return site, I would return to my room at the Ohalo Manor Motel and work on this book. Each day, with Jesus' help, I wrote about one of the seven churches in Christ's revelation to John. Each letter from Christ to these churches serves as the biblical and theological basis for His call for church reform. I completed the first part of all seven letters to the churches while I was in Israel waiting for Christ's return.

At six P.M. on January 25th, I made a final visit to the return site, facing my car toward the stage there. A spectacular full moon lit up the night sky. I opened the windows, turned on the interior lights, and started reading Scripture. As I read, the interior became the site of a furious windstorm. Then at six twenty-one, my wrist-alarm sounded for nineteen seconds and I looked a last time at the platform of the return site. I had not set the alarm, so I considered it as Christ's farewell to me at Daliyyot. I then started the car and headed back to my motel. As I passed the eastern hills, I said goodbye to the big fisherman statue that sits on a cliff overlooking the Sea of Galilee. As I drove along the coast, I looked awestruck at the full moon, lapping in the night air. After checking out of my room and paying my bill, I drove my rental car south to the Tel Aviv airport.

Jesus did not bodily return on January 25, 2005. However, He led in the writing of the first part of each chapter about His letters to the seven churches in chapters two and three of the book of Revelation. He showed me that He wanted His church reformed to become heavenly churches all over the world.

I asked God to let the light of Jesus Christ shine through me to the churches of the world. I asked Him to let the churches of the world illuminate their congregations with His holy light, to give all churches a renewed mission, and to let every member of every church take the light of Jesus Christ into the world. I asked Him to help the churches become heavenly churches all over our planet.

After I returned to North Carolina, the Lord led me to Lon Ackelson, Th.D., a Bible Institute instructor in California, to provide writing and editing assistance for *Is Your Church Heavenly?*. Both Dr. Ackelson and I trust that this book will bring glory to God and help each reader create a reflection of heaven in his or her church.

Introduction

John Henry Newman preached a sermon entitled *Holiness Necessary for Future Blessedness.* Part of his sermon introduces the heavenly church:

> Heaven then is not like this world; I will say what it is much more like—a church. For in a place of public worship no language of this world is heard; there are no schemes brought forward for temporal objects, great or small; no information how to strengthen our worldly interests, extend our influence, or establish our credit. These things indeed may be right in their way, so that we do not set our hearts upon them; still (I repeat), it is certain that we hear nothing of them in a church. Here we hear solely and entirely of God. We praise Him, worship Him, sing to Him, thank Him, confess to Him, give ourselves up to Him, and ask His blessing. And therefore, **a church is like heaven;** viz. because both in the one and the other, there is one single sovereign subject—religion—brought before us.[1]

As Jesus slowly moved with His disciples through the province of Perea on His way to Judea in the final weeks of His earthly ministry, He encountered a man who was eager to find out the requirements to join His disciples. In the tenth chapter of the Gospel of Mark (Mark 10:17–22; also found in Luke 18:18–24 and Matt. 19:16–22), we read about this encounter with a man rich in worldly possessions and outwardly righteous in obedience to God's Law. This young official, who may have been a synagogue leader (see Luke 18:18), was a man who was confident in his wealth and Jewish religion. However, he wondered if he could connect with

1

the disciples of Jesus Christ without having to give up too much.

When this rich fellow asked Jesus, "What must I do to inherit eternal life?", he expected a list of good works necessary for the result he sought. Jesus' answer met his expectations: "You know the commandments: 'Do not murder, do not commit adultery, do not steal, do not give false testimony, do not defraud, honor your father and mother.'

"'Teacher,' the man said, 'all these I have kept since I was a boy'" (Mark 10:17, 19–20). In other words, "It's a done deal to connect with You, Jesus, since obeying the fifth through the tenth Commandments are all You require of Your followers. Obedience to the Ten Commandments has been drilled into me, as it is to most Jewish men, since my boyhood."

Then Jesus shook up this smug young man by adding one more requirement to enter the kingdom of heaven. He added directions for the one who met the requirements for the six interpersonal commands of the Ten Commandments to do just one more good work. Jesus added, "Go, sell everything you have and give to the poor, and you will have treasure in heaven. Then come, follow me" (verse 21).

Jesus made it very clear that the riches of heaven have nothing to do with the riches of the world. If you want one, you cannot have the other. If you are connected to worldly riches, as the rich young man was, you have to disconnect from them in order to connect to heavenly riches.

Suppose Jesus commanded you to go and sell all that you have and give all the money from the sale to a mission who works with homeless poor people in your town or city. Afterward, your Lord and Master called you to serve Him as a missionary in a country within the 10–40 window (people groups never reached with the gospel) that is hostile to Christians.

- How would you react to the sale of all your possessions as the requirements to become a disciple of Christ and serve Him as a member of a faith-mission for the rest of your life?

- Could you put all of your trust in Jesus Christ and follow Him, not knowing where He would lead you, *after* giving control of everything you have and are to Him?

The answer to each of these questions for a committed Christian is not an always-easy yes. However, when we surrender the lordship of our lives to Jesus Christ, we give control of all our worldly possessions to Him. He always wants His followers emancipated from connections to anything that will not accompany them to heaven. Never forget how Peter the Apostle addressed believers: "Peter, an apostle of Jesus Christ, To God's elect, **strangers in the world…**" (1 Pet. 1:1).

Let us ask these same questions of our churches of today.

- Could our church leaders sell all of our church property and give all of the money to a homeless poor ministry in our community?

- Could they put all of their trust in Jesus Christ, not our pastoral team, to lead our congregation, and could they follow Christ's agenda for the church, not that of the church's spiritual leaders?

- Could these leaders let go of this world and its agenda and follow Christ and His agenda to develop a heavenly church?

Mark told us that the rich man went away unhappy and that "the disciples were amazed at his words" (Mark 10:24). Jesus' disciples believed that if you were rich in the world's goods, your riches would seldom stand between you and Christ. However, Jesus said they would, and this news amazed them because it seemed so unlikely.

This young rich man represents what many consider the ideal church member today—someone who offers the Church both money and worldly influence. To be honest, many of us would probably rather follow this rich man's decision not to sell everything he owned than to follow Christ if we had to actually give up everything we possessed and would never see it again to follow Him.

In this rich man, we see someone whom we might believe has the best of both heaven and earth—all the rights and privileges of religion and the financial fruits of the world. We see an appearance of God blessing financially those who are both rich and religious—what is called the "Prosperity Gospel." However, appearances can be courtesy of a satanic angel of light, and in this case, are.

Newman's sermon about heavenly churches so impelled me that whenever I had opportunities to minister as a lay pastor, I began preaching the concept of the Church as a reflection of heaven on earth. To close each heavenly church sermon, I told my congregation, "We are gathered together today as a priesthood of believers in Jesus Christ and we are joined by God the Father, God the Son, and God the Holy Spirit. How many of you want to reconvene this gathering in heaven someday?"

Hands waved heavenward whenever I asked this question.

After Jesus watched the exodus of the rich young man, He "said to His disciples, 'How hard it is for the rich to enter the kingdom of God!'

"The disciples were *amazed* at his words. But Jesus said again,

'Children, how hard it is to enter the kingdom of God! It is easier for a camel to go through the eye of a needle than for the rich to enter the kingdom of God.'

"The disciples were even more amazed, and said to each other, 'Who then can be saved?'

"Jesus looked at them and said, 'With man this is impossible, but not with God; all things are possible with God'" (Mark 10:23, 26–27).

The young rich man's problem was not money—it was about *control*. He could not give up control of his life and his earthly riches to follow Christ. His money gave him the freedom to go his own way and not *God's* way. He thought he could come to God on his *own* terms and went away sadly when he learned *God's* terms. What is even sadder, as he entered a tug-of-war between earthly and heavenly riches, he made the wrong choice with eternal consequences.

The obstacle that kept the young man from joining Jesus' disciples exists in many of our churches today. We often have the same control issue that he had: the senior pastor or the other spiritual leaders, who want to be in control of their church, enter into a tug-of-war with Jesus for this honor. However, the members and the spiritual leaders must yield to Jesus the leadership of our church if we are to become a heavenly church—a church where Christ reigns, the glory of God glows within, and the light of heaven shines into the world. We must let go of the tug-of-war rope and prepare our congregations to become heavenly churches. Such churches demonstrate the heart of Christ and put God's will first.

After I was saved in 1982, God laid on my heart, that He, through Jesus Christ, must be **first** in the lives of Christians. He also made it clear that I had a responsibility to make life **simple** and **right** (one *simple* way of salvation is the only *right* way to heaven;

heavenly churches are God's *simple* and *right* instruments for the consecration and sanctification of Christians). When Christ is in control of our lives, we can *never* hold that position! In fact, Jesus made it clear that positions among Christians are just the opposite of what they are in the world: "So the last will be first, and the first will be last" (Matt. 20:16).

Our churches must get their priorities straight and fix their eyes on heaven as Paul did: "Brothers, I do not consider myself yet to have taken hold of it. But one thing I do: Forgetting what is behind and straining toward what is ahead, I press on toward the goal to win the prize for which God has called me heavenward in Christ Jesus" (Phil. 3:13–14). We need to forget what is behind (not losing all memory of our sinful past, but leaving it behind us after it is confessed to God, as done with and settled) and strain toward what is ahead (as runners who draw upon all our remaining spiritual strength and stretch out toward the goal). Just as Christ sought to reform the seven churches of Asia in Revelation 2–3 so they would be heavenly churches, we need to let Him reform our churches toward the same goal.

Jesus' Call to Reform His Church Into a Heavenly Church

As part of Christ's revelation to His beloved Apostle John, He dictated seven letters to seven churches in Asia, and told what needed to be reformed—in the most part, *radically* reformed— before the result would be a heavenly church on earth.

Using Christ's letters in Revelation as a church evaluation guide, the following chapters of this book (chapters one through seven) depict seven different types of churches that Christ sought to reform to be heavenly churches. Then chapter eight brings together all the attributes of a heavenly church drawn from the previous seven chapters. It is our earnest prayer that each reader considers the characteristics of each of these seven churches of the Revelation to evaluate his or her local congregation. The following three brief outlines are introductory to what these seven churches look like to Christ.

Christ classifies each of these seven churches in a distinctive manner:

- **Orthodox**—This church (Ephesus) performed many good works for the Lord, but did not do so because of their love for Him, but because it was expected of Orthodox Christians.

- **Rich**—This church (Smyrna) ranks near the bottom by worldly standards, but their rich spiritual life ranks them near the top by heavenly standards.

- **True or False**—For most of the members of this church (Pergamum), Christ, not the minister or some church member, remains as the Head of the faithful congregation. However, some members of this church do not follow Christ, but satan.

- **Tolerant**—This church (Thyatira) has compromised God's Word on the issue of immoral lifestyles to appeal to worldly people.

- **Dead**—This church (Sardis) appears attractive on the outside but, on Sunday morning, there are either a few people in the pews, or there may be many people present but, no matter the number, they are all spiritually dead.

- **Faithful**—For this loving congregation (Philadelphia), Christ and all His teachings guide its worship, work, and mission.

- **Lukewarm**—This church (Laodicea) reflects the ways of the world and just goes through the motions of the Christian life.

  Which descriptive term best represents your local church?

Christ then makes the following requests of these seven congregations:

- **Remember, repent, and surrender**—Christ cries out to this congregation (Ephesus) to remember how far they fell, repent of their sin, and surrender to the lordship of Jesus Christ.

- **Be Faithful**—Christ encourages this church (Smyrna) to be brave even if they hear satan knocking at their door and not to fear any suffering for their faith.

- **Repent and Jettison**—Christ convicts this church (Pergamum) of tolerating false teachers who teach the sins of the flesh and calls them to oust all false teachers.

- **Repent!**—Christ calls this church (Thyatira) to repent of the sin of letting false teaching infiltrate the church and forsake the false for the true.

- **Wake Up!** Christ calls this church (Sardis) to wake up spiritually and remember the message from the Bible that they have ignored so long, repenting of their sin.

- **Be Protected.** Christ promises protection from a severe crisis that faces this church (Philadelphia) and encourages them to faithfully obey God's Word all the time.

- **Open Your Door**—Christ tells this group of professing Christians (Laodicea), "Let Me come in and save your lost members, then change you into a heavenly church."

Which request from Christ is being asked of the members of your local church?

In His letters, Christ offers rewards for the members of each church who overcome:

- **New Food**— Ephesus' overcomers will partake of the fruit of the tree of life that grows in the Garden of God in heaven.

- **New Life**— Smyrna's overcomers will live forever in God's great home after receiving the crown of eternal life.

- **New Name**— Pergamum's overcomers will receive a new name known only to them and Christ, learned at a wonderful banquet in the Messianic Kingdom.

- **New Clothes**— Thyatira's overcomers will discard the robes of death and put on the clean white linen of the citizens of heaven.

- **New Citizenship**— Sardis' overcomers will worship in this new city and become a leader in God's temple in heaven.

- **New Purpose**— Philadelphia's overcomers will be given co-regency duties over the nations on earth and satan during the Messianic Kingdom.

- **Seats in Heaven**—The overcomers from Laodicea will be seated in one of the heavenly seats right next to Jesus.

Which heavenly blessing awaits your local church and its members?

The Church needs a major reformation to become the heavenly church that John Newman visualized. As you read each chapter ahead, you will learn things about the seven churches of the Revelation that remind you of your own church. You will see the positive and negative characteristics, consequences, and rewards that Christ wants the members and leaders of each church to understand. As you learn the characteristics that set each of the seven churches of the Revelation apart, note the church that is most like your own and what reformation Christ says is needed for members of that church.

Note to the Reader

Please find a section at the end of each chapter called *Suggestions for the Local Church*. The information contained in these sections is gathered from other respected resources. Information on these resources can be found in the bibliography at the back of this book.

1

Orthodox Ephesus Church

THE MESSAGE TO EPHESUS

"To the angel of the church in Ephesus write:

"These are the words of him who holds the seven stars in his right hand and walks among the seven golden lampstands: I know your deeds, your hard work and your perseverance. I know that you cannot tolerate wicked men, that you have tested those who claim to be apostles but are not, and have found them false. You have persevered and have endured hardships for my name, and have not grown weary.

"Yet I hold this against you: You have forsaken your first love. Remember the height from which you have fallen! Repent and do the things you did at first. If you do not repent, I will come to you and remove your lampstand from its place. But you have this in your favor: You hate the practices of the Nicolaitans, which I also hate.

"He who has an ear, let him hear what the Spirit says to the churches. To him who overcomes, I will give the right to eat from the tree of life, which is in the paradise of God"
(Rev. 2:1–7).

The Background of Ephesus

Ephesus was the capital of the Roman province of Asia, located at the mouth of the Cayster River on the west coast of Asia Minor. Because of its fine harbor facilities and the roads that converged at that point, this city of more than 300,000 people became the most important commercial center of Roman Asia. It boasted numerous warehouses lining the banks of the river. Remains of an amphitheater can still be seen.

The city was most widely known for its temple of Artemis (Diana), one of the Seven Wonders of the World. When the first temple was constructed is not known. The structure standing in Paul's day was begun about 350 B.C. It measured 340 by 100 feet, and its 100 columns stood more than 55 feet high. The goddess Artemis was originally an Anatolian fertility deity who had become partially a Greek goddess. In addition to its religious significance, the temple also served both as a bank for the deposit and lending of money and as an asylum for fugitives.

On his third missionary journey, Paul spent almost three years in Ephesus (Acts 19), no doubt because of its strategic position as a radiating center for the dissemination of the gospel. Timothy was later stationed there as an apostolic representative, giving assistance to local church leaders (see 1 and 2 Tim.). Church Fathers indicate that the apostle John spent his last years in Ephesus, from which he wrote the Gospel of John, 1 John, 2 John, and 3 John, before being exiled to the Island of Patmos to write Revelation.

Part I: Jesus' Positive Evaluation of the Church at Ephesus

Notice that Jesus commends this church for seven very good things they have done:

I know (1) *your deeds,* (2) *your hard work, and* (3) *your perseverance. I know that* (4) *you cannot tolerate wicked men, that* (5) *you have tested those who claim to be apostles but are not, and have found them false.* (3) *You have persevered,* (6) *endured hardships for My name, and* (7) *you have not grown weary.* (Note that number 3 is stated twice. These Christians are about as patient as a person can get.)

Another feather in their cap was: *But you have this in your favor:* (8) *You hate the practices of the Nicolaitans, which I also hate* (Rev. 2:6). They abhorred the practice of the Nicolaitans just as Jesus did. Now just who were these *Nicolaitans?* In the first century, "Nicolaitans" was the label given to a heretical sect that considered it lawful to eat food sacrificed to idols, to join in idolatrous worship, and to believe that God did not create the universe. This aberrant sect apparently taught that spiritual liberty gave them license to practice idolatry and immorality. Commending the members and leaders of the Ephesus Church, Christ noted how their heart against worldly and apostate things was just like His heart.

Jesus had eight positive things to say about the church at Ephesus. They were Christians (1) who performed good deeds, (2) worked hard for the Lord, (3) were patient, (4) did not tolerate false teachers, (5) tested those who wanted to teach and preach, (6) suffered for their faith, (7) did not give up when oppressed, and (8) hated worldly and apostate things. However, notice the beginning of the sentence Jesus gave for the last positive characteristic He described (*"But you have this in your favor"*). It begins with "But." This contrasting conjunction means that this eighth positive feature was in sharp contrast with a negative feature that Jesus had just stated in His letter to the Ephesus Church. Although Jesus had described a number of instances of commendable Christian conduct to describe the Christians in the Ephesus Church, just before He concluded this letter, He made it clear that no matter how many good works a Christian does, they are worthless if they are not performed because of his love for his Lord!

Part II: Jesus' Negative Evaluation of the Church at Ephesus

Jesus' verdict for those in the church at Ephesus was that, no matter how the members and leaders had been living fine Christian lives outwardly, they had a great sinful defect: *"You have forsaken your first love"* (Rev. 2:4). "You do not love Me now as you did when you first accepted Me as your personal Savior, and you have chosen to abandon that love!"

Jesus raised only one objection against the Ephesus Church but it caused all the positive traits commended by Him to pale into insignificance. They had "forsaken" (willfully turned their back on) their first love for Christ; as a consequence, they did not express the love they had for Christ right after they were saved and delivered from the spiritual death penalty of sin. Just what did that "first love" involve?

Think back, if you can, to how much you loved Jesus when you were first born-again into the family of God. Now picture a lamb that manages to get lost from the flock and is on its own. The lamb does not realize that it is in a perilous place where camouflaged foxes are silently closing in on it. The lamb bleats repeatedly for its mother, hoping to find her over the next rise. However, its journey takes it further from the flock. Then, just as the sly predators prepare to leap at the defenseless lamb, the shepherd spies the lost lamb. He uses his staff to strike the leaping animals and then scoops up the frightened lamb.

How much will that lamb love its shepherd once it is taken back to the loving care of its mother and the safety of the flock and the shepherd watching over it? (The *first love* of a lamb for a loving shepherd is demonstrated when it submits to its shepherd unconditionally and selflessly.)

How much would a sinner, who realized that he had no hope in the world, love the Good Shepherd once, after committing himself to the Good Shepherd, he was taken back to the safety of the family of God and the Good Shepherd watching over him 24/7? (Submitting to his Shepherd unconditionally and selflessly demonstrates the *first love* of a sinner saved by the Good Shepherd.)

First love for Christ is the love we have for Him when we repent of our sins and accept Him as our Savior. It is the selfless, unconditional *agape* (New Testament Greek word for "sacrificial love") that we demonstrate to the One who saved us from the penalty of our sins—not because of anything we did but because of His own perfect *agape* toward us. We demonstrate our *first agape* for Christ in the following five ways:

1. We are enthusiastic about sharing our faith and we cannot wait to tell others about what Christ means to us.

2. We seek God's will before all major decisions of life because we are surrendered to the lordship of Christ.

3. We study and internalize the Word of God because we are excited about growing spiritually as we discover wonderful things in the Bible, our textbook for living.

4. We pray regularly because we want to stay in contact with God so He can direct our lives.

5. We confess our sins because we hate to do anything to displease our wonderful Savior.

In other words, you Christians in the Ephesus Church are doing good things, working hard, showing patience, accepting persecution, not tolerating evil people, not giving up, and keeping satan's angels from teaching in your church. Your heart against worldly and apostate things is just like Christ's heart. However, you have no enthusiasm for a closer walk with Christ. If you did, you would be excited about sharing your testimony about Him, seeking God's will before major decisions, studying and internalizing the Word of God, praying regularly, and confessing your sins. These are all things that are demonstrated by those who have *first love* for Christ. Sadly, the love that the Ephesian believers had for Christ when they were born again had been extinguished by the 90s of the first century (the decade when John wrote Revelation). Paul warned the elders of Ephesus in Acts 20:27–31 about this falling away after he left them for the last time.

Jesus wants the Christians in the Ephesus Church to realize that their orthodox Christian lives that lack enthusiasm for a closer walk with Christ are a product of their old nature. He wants all of them to return to their first love for Him. For that to happen, they must dethrone their old nature from the helm of their lives.

"Orthodox (traditional religious) works," that were noticeable in Ephesus, were the fruits of *duty to* Christ instead of *love for* Him. Good works were done thus in the strength of the old nature instead of the grace of the new nature. This is why Jesus considered this sin so grievous: good things were being done in the strength of the old sin nature of Christians; thus satan controlled these believers as their devious angel of light, leading them to do all kinds of pious things. Satan then kept them ignorant of their real master as long as he could.

All of the members and leaders of the Ephesus Church left their first love for Jesus. Jesus made no exceptions, as He did in later letters to the seven churches of Asia. He indicted *every* member and leader of the Ephesus Church in the late first century for this sin. This church performed many good works for the Lord, but did not do so because of their love for Him, but simply because it was expected of Orthodox Christians.

Go back to the beginning of this chapter and reread Revelation 2:1–7. You will read about the eight positive and one negative features of the Ephesus Church. Now take a brief period to answer the following four questions as they relate to the Ephesus Church. Finally, answer the fifth question about your local church. Check Y for yes, N for no, CD for cannot determine, and DK for do not know. (Check the answers under this exercise only after you have answered each question as best you can.)

1-Does the worship of members of the Ephesus Church please Christ?
__Y __N __CD __DK
2-Does the work of members of the Ephesus Church please Christ?
__Y __N __CD __DK
3-Does the witness of members of the Ephesus Church please Christ?
__Y __N __CD __DK
4-What about the Ephesus Church displeases Christ?

_____

5-Which positives and/or negative about the Ephesus Church are present in your local church?

_____

(Answers: 1-CD [nothing is said about worship], 2-Y [hard work], 3-Y [suffered as witnesses], 4-They had lost their first love for Christ, 5-Answers will vary.)

Losing One's First Love in a Church of Today

I learned firsthand on my trip to Israel during the first month of 2005 of the sin of losing one's first love for Christ. I went to Capernaum on Wednesday morning, searching for a place of worship there. I discovered a Catholic church with glass walls and ceiling. Interested in investigating this unusual structure, I saw a short wall surrounding the church and through an opened gate in the wall, I climbed several stairs that led to the doors of the church. I then made a self-guided tour and discovered an inscription on a glass display board underneath the church, indicating that this church was built over the ruins of the first Christian church in Israel. (I knew that this claim by the Roman Catholic Church was not substantiated by archeology, but the house was likely that of a first century fisherman, which Peter and many others were. It may have been Peter's home, but there was no certainty that it was.) Through a glass floor in the center of the sanctuary, one can look through to what is labeled as "Peter's house—the first Christian church in Israel" (even if Peter's house could be located, it would not be the first Christian church in Israel, since the first Christian church in Israel was the temple in Jerusalem where Peter served as senior pastor).

After I sat down, I bowed my head to thank God for allowing me to get so close to New Testament times here in Capernaum. I heard the door open and looked up to see a nun enter the sanctuary, give the sign of the cross, and begin dusting the pews. I asked her if a local congregation from Tiberius met in this church.

"No," she replied. "Only Jews live in Tiberius now."

"Is this church just a tourist stop or is it used for Catholic masses?" I asked.

She informed me that tourists could reserve the church for services during each week through the church's booking agent in

Jerusalem.

"Are any services scheduled for this week?" I asked hopefully.

"Yes," she replied. "A tour group will worship here today at eleven o'clock."

"May I stay and worship with them?" I asked.

She ignored me and resumed her work.

Well, she did not say no, and since it was ten thirty, I decided to stay.

After the nun finished cleaning, she laid out a number of white robes and prepared the elements for the Eucharist on a long table.

At eleven o'clock, I was surprised to see the door open to admit fourteen priests. Following the clergy, about thirty tourists filed into the pews. Each priest put on a white robe and sat in a chair either behind or beside the communion table. The tourists, nun, and I filled the side of the church that faced the Sea of Galilee.

One of the priests stood and began giving a message from John 21:4–11. This passage of Scripture described the time after Jesus' resurrection when seven of His disciples spent a full night of fishing and never caught a single fish in their lowered net at any time during the night—the time when fish rise to the surface to feed. Then, in the morning—when fish go to the lower depths of the lake and fisherman would never go fishing for them—the resurrected Jesus commanded His disciples to cast their net on the *other* side of the boat. Now, normally, fishing from *any* side of the boat would be useless in the morning hours. However, after the disciples obeyed Jesus, they had so many fish that they could not haul in their net! One hundred and fifty-three large fish filled their net. Only a miracle could account for such a catch!

Once I realized that I was looking out on the water where that long-ago fishing expedition actually happened, a lump filled my throat and I did not "hear" any of the rest of the message. My attention swerved from the speaker to the glass walls that looked out onto the Sea of Galilee. I was surprised to see forks of lightning coming from dark clouds in the distance that seemed to be moving toward the church.

As booming thunderclaps resounded throughout the sanctuary, we could all see the thundershowers moving across the Sea of Galilee toward the church. Soon the heavens opened over us. Lightning lit up the church and was closely followed by thunder. During one pause between a thunder roll, an insistent pounding could be heard on the door of the church. When the nun answered the door, some rain-soaked tourists stepped inside, urgently requesting shelter from the storm.

The nun incredulously told the visitors that they could not come in because a service was in progress. She escorted them back into the downpour, then locked the fence gate behind them.

I could not believe what I had just witnessed! In refusing shelter for people in desperate need, she did not show any love for Christ who commanded His followers to be servants (see Mark 10:43; John 13:14–17). She didn't even show normal *humanity* to those who sought shelter from a dangerous storm! Even if the nun was under orders not to admit anyone after the service began, such a heartless order should have admitted to exceptions in a time like this.

After that unexpected display of coldness to the needy by the nun, the priest who gave the Bible lesson served the Eucharist first to the priests; then he served the tourists and the nun after each came to the altar. The mass then ended, and everyone but I stayed inside to tour the facility and to shelter from the storm. After a brief survey of the building's contents, I went outside in the pouring rain. I could not stay in a church that was so inhumane.

No Lost First Love in the Jerusalem Church

If strangers had come to Jerusalem to the temple, which held the first Christian church, to seek shelter from the elements, Jesus' disciples would never have turned them away like the nun did in the twenty-first century. Jesus' disciples would have demonstrated their first love for Christ by treating strangers just as Jesus treated them.

Notice what Dr. Luke reported in the book of Acts about the Early Church of the first century: "They devoted themselves to the apostles' teaching and to the fellowship, to the breaking of bread and to prayer. Everyone was filled with awe, and many wonders and miraculous signs were done by the apostles. All the believers were together and had everything in common. Selling their possessions and goods, they gave to anyone as he had need. Every day they continued to meet together in the temple courts. They broke bread in their homes and ate together with glad and sincere hearts, praising God and enjoying the favor of all the people. And the Lord added to their number daily those who were being saved" (Acts 2:42–47). Luke described a bunch of people who evidenced their first love for Christ.

Jewish people were welcomed in the churches of the first century. Other Jewish people who found the Messiah wanted to show their fellow-Jews how to discover Him as their own Messiah/Savior. Those with needs had their needs met by the early Christians. Strangers would have found a warm welcome in Christian churches in Israel.

Christian churches in Israel were open to the lost by those who fell in love with Christ. Sadly, the Israeli church of our time was not. If any one of the tourists seeking shelter from the rainstorm was spiritually lost, they would connect Christianity to how they were treated when they had a distinct need for safety that a church could have met and yet chose not to.

The Christian church in Israel was a welcoming place for anyone who wanted to seek spiritual shelter within it. The successor church was an orthodox institution that did have a formal church service going on, but the service was only open to tourists who had sought and received permission before being part of the group going there. If someone came to the church doors with special needs after the service was underway, they would be turned away, for a love for Christ's command for Christians to demonstrate sacrificial love to others was not in evidence.

Sometimes It Can Be Hard to Demonstrate Our First Love for Christ

On Friday morning, I went to the return site at Daliyyot (see the prologue) and mounted the stage there. I discovered that the wind on the stage was so strong that I thought it might carry me away. As it blew harder, I raised my arms in ecstasy, wondering if God's Spirit would lift me up to meet Jesus in the air.

Then, I noticed a hitchhiker on the roadside intently watching me. The wind bent the tops of palm trees and stirred up dust. My observer, though windswept, stopped to observe my strange movements on the stage.

I then lowered my arms and then raised them again several times, just as if I was doing calisthenics. I soon noticed my audience fighting the wind as he moved on so I concluded my impromptu exercise session.

Sometimes it is difficult to live a spiritual life in a physical world, is it not? My first love for Christ was certainly not in evidence when the only enthusiasm I demonstrated was my energetic calisthenics to a possible unbeliever.

Do you remember when you left your mountaintop experience

of salvation or a later mountaintop experience as a Christian (perhaps after a Christian summer camp during your youth) for the valley of Christian living below? Consider the descent you experienced or, if this has not yet been your experience, one that is common for Christians after a spiritual-mountaintop experience:

Descent from the Spiritual Mountain

We cannot live on the mountaintop of salvation or a spiritual-mountaintop experience as believers. We have to return to the "valley," a location somewhere below the mountain we have been on, where we live along with other inhabitants of our planet. However, we can continue to be motivated by our love for Christ as we descend the mountain of salvation or a later mountaintop experience to the valley of Christian living. Yet, many Christians forsake their first love for Christ as they return to the valley. In fact, there are three obstacles where one's first love can be forsaken in the valley of Christian living:

- First, we often encounter the DIFFERENT INTERESTS obstacle. Here is where we find that our friends begin to notice that we have different interests than they. We feel uncomfortable around them and they around us. As we seek to raise the comfort area of our unsaved friends, we lower our level of love for Christ. A selfless love for Christ is not demonstrated by pleasing unbelievers who want us to be like them, but only by pleasing Christ. To keep our friends happy, we forsake our first love for Christ.

- We may overcome the first obstacle, but then we face the second obstruction: the TOUGH QUESTIONS obstacle. At this stumbling block, our friends and acquaintances start to ask us tough questions about Christianity, because they are uncomfortable with it. Wanting to please our friends, we develop answers we think they want to hear to the tough questions they ask us. Our weak answers keep us from being recognized as more than nominal Christians. We demonstrate no love for Christ's command for Christians to share the gospel. Nominal Christianity does not demonstrate a selfless, unconditional love for Christ. To answer our friends' objections, we forsake our first love for Christ.

- We may overcome the first two obstacles, but then we face the third obstruction: the CHANGED BEHAVIOR obstacle. When we come to this stumbling block, we hear from our friends and acquaintances, who want to proactively change our behavior so we will not offend them. If we accept any of their proposed changes, then we must dilute our Christianity. Where is our first love for Christ? It is not in evidence. We are just as the Christians Jesus addressed in His first letter to the seven churches in Revelation 2. To implement any of our friends' proposed changes, we forsake our first love for Christ.

The same three obstacles in the valley exist whether it is our first time down after salvation or a later time when we descend from a spiritual mountaintop experience. Those who lose their first love for Christ after a mountaintop experience do so in this valley or in one very much like it.

Part III: Jesus' Corrective Command to the Church at Ephesus

We have considered the problem of losing one's first love for Christ. Now we need to look at how a person who has lost his or her first love for Christ can find it again.

According to Christ in Revelation 2:5, there are three important steps to follow:

Step One: *Remember* How Far You Have Fallen

"Remember the height from which you have fallen!" (Rev. 2:5a).

Christ told the members and leaders of the church at Ephesus that, no matter how orthodox they were in services to the Lord, they needed to measure how far they had fallen from their initial first love for Christ.

How far had they fallen? They fell *from* the *love for Christ* motivating them to be enthusiastic about sharing their faith, seeking God's will in decisions, studying God's Word, praying regularly, and confessing their sins under Christ's control. They fell *to* the *duty for Christ* to motivate their orthodox Christian behavior of hard work, patience, suffering, and intolerance of false teachers and teaching. This duty was really under the control of satan, who wears his best Christ-disguise.

They fell from Christ's control to satan's control—as far down as a believer could fall without being a slave of satan for the rest of his or her life. Satan cannot *possess* a born-again Christian, but he can and does *influence* them when they are not submitted to Christ's control.

Let's take a trip down salvation's memory lane and see what we can learn from the early days of our Christian lives so we can get a

26

better fix on how far we can fall from our first love for Christ:

1. **Remember** that when you were first born again, you did everything as a new Christian because of your great love for Christ, who died to pay the penalty for all your sins. Your love for your Savior was alive and well on day one of your spiritual life.

2. **Remember** as a new believer when you had that "first enthusiasm"? You were enthusiastic to let others know about your newfound faith so they could fall in love with the Lover of their souls, too. Your love for your Savior motivated you to share your faith in the first days of your spiritual life.

3. **Remember** that first special expression of love for the church community. You expressed love to your fellow brothers and sisters in Christ because you had such a great love for the Lover of your soul. Members of your spiritual family were very special to you during your early life as a believer for your first love to Christ was what motivated you then.

4. **Remember** that when people are born again, they often experience a spiritual high:

    - They pray as often as they can.
    - They go to church whenever the doors are open for public services.
    - They study the Bible morning and night. They may even start reading through it in a year.
    - They gladly share meals and fellowship with other Christians.
    - They seek opportunities to witness for Jesus.

- They seek opportunities to serve Jesus within their church.

5. **Remember** when you first noticed that your motivation for Christian service changed from *love for* Christ to *duty and obligation to* Him. Think back to your first service opportunity that you considered a burden, not a blessing. Perhaps you worked hard on a church project and when you received no affirmation for the excellent work you did, you forgot that all glory was to go to the Lord and none to man (see Isa. 42:8).

Step Two: Repent of Your Sin!

After remembering how far you have fallen from your first love for Christ, you realize that you need to *"Repent"* (Rev. 2:5b). Christ told the church at Ephesus that they needed to repent of their sin of serving him out of obligation and duty (including the sin of letting their old natures control them to demonstrate orthodox Christian deeds). The Apostle Paul told the believers at Corinth what repentance involved: "Now I am happy, not because you were made sorry, but because *your sorrow led you to repentance.* For you became sorrowful as God intended and so were not harmed in any way by us" (2 Cor. 7:9). Paul was pleased that the sorrow of the sinning Corinthian Christians for their grievous sin (they regretted their condoning of immoral conduct among close Christian family members and were sad that they did something to displease their loving heavenly Father) led them to repent. In Revelation 2:1–7, Christ will be pleased if the sorrow of the sinning Ephesians or churches like them leads them to repent of their sin of losing their first love for Christ.

Repentance (the Greek word *metanoieo*) involves a "change" (*meta*) of "mind" (*noieo*). It means a fixed change of your mind to *turn from* the path of sin (confessing to God that you were on the wrong path and now forsake it) and to *turn to* the path of Christ (confessing to Christ that you surrender to His control over your life). To repent of sin after being a Christian is described by the Apostle John in 1 John 1:9—*"If we confess our sins, He is faithful and just and will forgive us our sins and purify us from all unrighteousness."* If we confess our sins (repent of the control of our old nature and what we did under its control, forsaking our sinful behavior), then God will forgive us and purify us from the confessed sins (remove the control of our old nature and the stain of the sin that is confessed to Him).

Step Three: Surrender to the Lordship of Jesus Christ

After repenting of the sin of yielding to the old nature, it is time to *"do the things you did at first"* (Rev. 2:5c)—surrender to the lordship of Jesus Christ and thus return to the motivation of your great love for Him in all that you do to serve Him. This is the third (final) step back to the first love you had for Christ. Once you take this step, you find your first love again. Notice the different ways the Bible labels this surrender:

1. *"Clothe yourselves with the Lord Jesus Christ, and do not think about how to gratify the desires of the sinful nature"* (Rom. 13:14).

2. "You were taught, with regard to your former way of life, to *put off your old self,* which is being corrupted by its deceitful desires; to be made new in the attitude of your minds; and to *put on the new self,* created

to be like God in true righteousness and holiness"
(Eph. 4:22–24).

3.   "Those controlled by the sinful nature cannot please
      God. *You, however, are controlled not by the sinful
      nature but by the Spirit,* if the Spirit of God lives in you.
      And if anyone does not have the Spirit of Christ, he
      does not belong to Christ" (Rom. 8:8–9).

4.   "I put this in human terms because you are weak in
      your natural selves. *Just as you used to offer the parts of
      your body in slavery to impurity and to ever-increasing
      wickedness, so now offer them in slavery to righteousness
      leading to holiness"* (Rom 6:19).

The church members and leaders at Ephesus and at any
churches like it need to take to heart the three steps noted to find
and then return to their first love for Christ:

REMEMBER
REPENT
SURRENDER.

To find the love one had when one was first born again
involves surrender to the lordship of Christ. When this surrender
occurs, these believers return to the wonders of Christ's love as
the motivation for all they do. The church that is composed of such
believers reflects heaven and is "a heavenly church."

Any church that imitates the one at Ephesus must have its
members return to their lives when they were first born again so
they can be a church impelled by Christ's love, not obligation or
duty.

If you look at your church and do not see an exciting love for

Jesus Christ motivating all that is done there, then ask God to lay it on the hearts of the members and leaders of your congregation to return to the time when they were born from above and surrender to the lordship of Christ. For professing Christians who do not possess Christ within, pray that they will be open to their need to be born again. Pray that God will make each person sensitive to serving Him out of a heart of love for Him, and reject service for any other reason.

Part IV: How Jesus Encouraged Overcomers of the Church at Ephesus

"To him who overcomes, I will give the right to eat from the tree of life, which is in the paradise of God" (Rev. 2:7). This means that the victor, the one who surrenders to Christ's lordship, will have all the rights and privileges of a citizen of heaven. Overcomers at Ephesus will be richly blessed in heaven one day. They will partake of the fruit of the tree of life (the same tree that grew in the Garden of Eden) that grows in the Garden of God in heaven, as they enter a blessed state similar to that enjoyed by Adam and Eve before their fall from grace.

Now, what happens to the believer who sinned like those at Ephesus and died without finding and returning to his first love for Christ? The Bible says that he is a true citizen of heaven but "will suffer loss; he himself will be saved, but only as one escaping through the flames" (1 Cor. 3:15). The "flames" are those that burned up wood, hay, and stubble good works at the Judgment Seat of Christ for Christians (see vv. 12–13). Orthodox Christian behavior, motivated by satan, will be burned up at that judgment.

Whereas overcomers will be rewarded in heaven, those who do not overcome the loss of their first love for Christ will go to the same destination but receive no reward there.

"He who has an ear, let him hear what the Spirit says to the churches" (Rev 2:7).

The members of Christ's Church need to return to their first love for Christ.

Suggestions for the Local Church

We have seen what it means when our first love for Christ is forsaken and how we can restore it again by (step one) remembering how far we fell, (step two) repenting of the fall we have recalled, and then (step 3) surrendering to the lordship of Christ. If anything will help a Christian, without first love for Christ, take these restorative steps, it is a short-term mission trip. Those who have gone on short-term mission trips can light a spiritual fire in a church that will consume any lethargy or extinguished first-love for Christ in the pews and rouse your church to new spiritual life.

Short-Term Mission Project at Appalachia Service Project

We came to Panther, West Virginia.

We were a group of professing Christians from Texas, North Carolina, and Minnesota.

We worked to refurbish mobile homes during the day (building a retaining wall behind each mobile home and adding underpinning to it), our large group divided into small groups who each worked on a mobile home. After our work project, we reassembled, sang, and worshipped together each evening. We slept thirty to a room in a local public elementary school.

We were on a short-term mission trip to Appalachia in the summer of 1997.

We gathered outside the school cafeteria for devotions on Thursday morning. This was our fifth day of lots of hard work, not enough sleep, small portions in all meals, no TV, no phones, no privacy, lots of new experiences, and making many new friends.

The clouds hung low in the hollow that morning, and we could barely see the top of the school.

All ninety of us formed a circle and held hands; then one of the high school students said the opening prayer.

Following the prayer, another high school student started the CD player. The valley filled with the sound of *Amazing Grace* played by bagpipes.

After the song, one of the young people read the passage in the Gospel of John about Nicodemus learning about being born again (John 3:1–8).

As a lay-preacher, I was asked to undertake the job of leading my work-team. I told all the work-teams that after being born again, Nicodemus became a different person, noting the following significant differences in his life after he encountered Jesus:

- **He changed from spiritually lost to found** by his Savior, thus changing his final destination from hell to heaven.

- **He took risks for Jesus.** When he sought an audience with Jesus at night, he risked his position in the Sanhedrin—spiritual leaders who hated Jesus.

- **He orally defended Jesus** in the Sanhedrin after they demanded Jesus' arrest in the temple where He was teaching the people contrary to Judaism.

- **He displayed his great love for Jesus** by helping Joseph of Arimathea take Jesus' body down from the cross and carrying Him to Joseph's garden tomb.

I made it clear after this week in the hills of West Virginia that each person was different from what we were when we arrived. We had all changed. We needed to go back to our churches and speak up for Jesus just as Nicodemus did. We needed to take Christ from this place and carry His mission into our communities.

Like Nicodemus, some of the professing Christian workers were born again during this mission trip. Many others returned to our first love for Jesus, surrendering every part of our lives to His lordship over them. We returned to our home churches with a newfound love for Jesus Christ and a new enthusiasm for His work.

Summer Ministry Program

This week in West Virginia was one when we worked for the Appalachia Service Project (ASP). ASP is a home repair and home-building ministry. Through this ministry, volunteers and ASP staff repair and build homes for low-income families in rural Central Appalachia. ASP's goal is to make homes warmer, safer, and drier, while offering transformational experiences for volunteers and homeowners alike.

Each year, ASP achieves its goal with the assistance of nearly 15,000 volunteers. The Summer Ministry Program is especially valuable for high school youth groups and their adult advisors. ASP also offers year-round service opportunities for college groups, family groups, individuals, and couples at their Housing Service Centers.

Pastors and other church staff members might want to consider the Summer Ministry Program for staff members. According to the ASP website, to be a member of the Summer Ministry Program staff is to be challenged! It is also to accept a very demanding, yet extremely rewarding position.

For more information on the Appalachia Service Project, please go to *www.asphome.org.*

Short-Term Mission Ministries

You have learned here about just one short-term mission group for your consideration. Now, it is up to you to connect with this or another short-term mission organization so you can get an opportunity to lead people in another country to accept Christ as their Savior and have a part in planting a new church in a neighborhood. You may also be involved in helping other people who need housing. Once a believer goes on a short-term mission, his or her life will never be the same!

If you have to admit that you have lost your first love for Jesus, then find it by going on a short-term mission trip this summer. If there are members of your church who just go through the motions, give them an opportunity to change their lives and the lives of other lethargic Christians at your church. I have never met anyone who went on such a trip who said the mission trip was an uneventful time in his or her life and the person had not fallen in love again with Jesus.[1]

A short-term mission trip will revolutionize the lives of Christians who connect with it. Whether your first love for Christ is lost or present, whenever you can become involved in an opportunity to demonstrate a servant's heart, you are simply following the example of your Savior and Lord. May God lead those who are reading this book to emulate the One who served you to the point of dying for you.

2
Rich Smyrna Church
THE MESSAGE TO SMYRNA

"To the angel of the church in Smyrna write:

"These are the words of him who is the First and the Last, who died and came to life again. I know your afflictions and your poverty — yet you are rich! I know the slander of those who say they are Jews and are not, but are a synagogue of Satan. Do not be afraid of what you are about to suffer. I tell you, the devil will put some of you in prison to test you, and you will suffer persecution for ten days. Be faithful, even to the point of death, and I will give you the crown of life.

"He who has an ear, let him hear what the Spirit says to the churches. He who overcomes will not be hurt at all by the second death" (Rev. 2:8–11).

The Background of Smyrna

Smyrna was designed by Alexander the Great and built by his successors, Antigonus and Lysimachus, near the site of the ancient city of the same name (which had been destroyed by the Lydians 400 years before Alexander's time).

Smyrna was located on the same site as the modern city of

Izmir, Turkey, at the southeast edge of the Gulf of Smyrna. The city curved around the edge of the bay at the base of the 525-foot Mount Pagus, its splendid acropolis. Its streets were excellently paved and drawn at right angles. One of them was known as the "Street of Gold" and ran from west to east, curving around the lower slopes of Mount Pagus. This famous street was lined with fine buildings and at each end was a temple. Probably the temple of Zeus stood at the western end and the temple of the mother goddess Cybele Sipylene (patron of the city) at the eastern end. The city had several squares, a public library, numerous temples, and other public buildings.

While Smyrna contested with Ephesus and Pergamum the rank, "First of Asia," some of her coins defined her rank as "First of Asia in beauty and size." Her prestige was also enhanced by her claim to have been the birthplace of Homer. In John's day the population may have approached 200,000.

Tiberius granted the city permission to erect a temple in honor of the Roman emperor and senate. John probably referred to the pagan rites in this temple in his letter to the church in Smyrna, where Christians faced intense persecution for refusing to worship the emperor of Rome.

Compare the Letters to Smyrna and Ephesus

Does this letter of Christ sound anything like the letter He wrote to the Ephesus Church? In that letter, which we examined in chapter one, Christ praised a number of things that the members and leaders were doing to please God, but He had one huge issue against them: they had lost their first love for Him. Now carefully check out the letter before you now, and determine how many issues you can find that Christ had against those in the Smyrna Church.

You searched for something that is nowhere to be found in this letter. Christ said *nothing* negative about those in the Smyrna Church! He did the same in His next-to-last letter, which was addressed to the Philadelphia Church. The other five letter recipients read one or more negative statements from the Writer. However, His only direct comment about the behavior of the Smyrna believers was positive, and we can infer from His counsel a second praiseworthy statement. He evaluated them as being spiritually rich believers and encouraged them to stand up for Him as they faced enemies of their faith—even at the cost of their lives. However, even though Christ said nothing negative about the believers in the Smyrna Church, He said nothing *positive* about their enemies.

Part I: Jesus' Positive Evaluation of the Church at Smyrna

Notice the following five features of this uplifting letter to the Smyrna Church:

1. *"I know your afflictions and your poverty—yet you are rich!"* Christ knew that these believers were not well off financially and faced troubles from the enemies of Christ. However, though these Christians faced troubles from their spiritual enemies and were poor in this world's riches, their spiritual coffers overflowed! That they were spiritually rich was the only direct statement of praise delivered in this letter. This means that their consecration, worship, service, and witness were dynamic features of their lives and that they were growing spiritually each day through Bible study and prayer.

2. ***"I know the slander of those who say they are Jews
   and are not, but are a synagogue of Satan."*** Christ
   highlighted a group within the city of Smyrna who
   claimed to be God-fearing Jews. However, no matter
   what external title this group of persecutors of
   Christians claimed, it was counterfeit. Their Creator
   branded them as members of the family of satan. They
   may have been Jews in *name,* but they were not Jews
   in *heart* (descended by faith from Abraham).

3. ***"Do not be afraid of what you are about to suffer."***
   The flock of God in Smyrna was well acquainted
   with suffering for faith in the Good Shepherd.
   Demands for emperor worship plus a large and
   actively hostile Jewish population made it extremely
   difficult to live there as a Christian. However, Christ
   gently encouraged them to trust in Him, no matter
   the consequences. As they were about to face more
   suffering for their faith, Christ said, "Don't be afraid
   of anything," because He would be with them and
   strengthen them to handle any oppression.

4. ***I tell you, the devil will put some of you in prison to test
   you, and you will suffer persecution for ten days.*** Christ
   prophesied that the believers in Smyrna needed to
   listen carefully to Him, because they would soon face
   severe persecution. Some of them would be thrown
   into prison just because of their stand for Christ.
   Satan would test these Christians like he tested Job.
   This time of trouble was to last "ten days." However
   this period of time is to be measured (ten literal *days*
   or ten *day-years),* we note that it is a *limited* time
   of intense trouble, but their persecution would be
   unlimited.

40

5. *Be faithful, even to the point of death, and I will give you the crown of life.* Persecution of believers in Smyrna was even to martyrdom. Christ gently encouraged them to be faithful to Him, even if it meant the loss of their lives. Those who paid the ultimate price also won the ultimate spiritual prize: the crown of life in heaven (see Jas. 1:12).

The first feature Christ *stated* about the believers in Smyrna was their **spiritual richness**. Their consecration, worship, service, and witness were dynamic features of their lives, and they grew spiritually each day. Spiritual richness is a quality of the members of a heavenly church.

The second feature that Christ *implied* about the believers in Smyrna was their faithfulness to the Lord under oppression. They were faithful to lose their lives rather than their faith. Willingness to suffer persecution for your faith is a quality of the members of a heavenly church.

This, the second church of Asia addressed by Christ, was not only filled with members and leaders who were spiritually rich, but who were harshly persecuted because of their faith. The Romans who worshipped pagan gods and their emperor considered Christians the off scouring of the world—not principally because of their faith in Christ, but because they refused to worship the emperor of Rome. Such a refusal was seen as a slap in the face of the ruler of Rome—something no good Roman citizen would ever do; thus, every good citizen of Rome considered Christians worthy of persecution.

The word "Smyrna" is related to the word "myrrh," which in turn is symbolic of death. Smyrna's history has been one of successive sackings, fires, and destructions. Polycarp, one of the most famous of the earlier martyrs, was Bishop of Smyrna. This city is the only one of the seven addressed by Christ that is still in flourishing condition. It is the site of the modern city of Izmir, Turkey.

One of Smyrna's main streets in the first century, lined with fine buildings, was known as the "Street of Gold." At each end of this street was a temple. Since Christians were an outlawed, persecuted religion in Smyrna, their church meetings in this city would have been in secret areas that may have been tunnels (catacombs) below the city. The Smyrna Church ranks near the bottom by worldly standards, but their rich spiritual life ranks them near the top by heavenly standards.

Go back to the beginning of this chapter and reread
Revelation 2:8–11. You will read about the five positive
features of the Smyrna Church. Now take a brief period
to answer the following four questions as they relate to
the Smyrna Church. Finally, answer the fifth question
about your local church. Check Y for yes, N for no, CD
for cannot determine, and DK for do not know. (Check
the answers under this exercise only after you have
answered each question as best you can.)

**1-Does the worship of members of the
Smyrna Church please Christ?
__Y __N __CD __DK
2-Does the work of members of the Smyrna
Church please Christ?
__Y __N __CD __DK
3-Does the witness of members of the Smyrna
Church please Christ?
__Y __N __CD __DK
4-What about the Smyrna Church
displeases Christ?**

_____

**5-Which positives and/or negative about the
Smyrna Church are present in your local church?**

_____

(Answers: 1-Y, 2-Y [spiritually rich], 3-Y [spiritually rich], 4-
Nothing, 5-Answers will vary.)

A Contemporary Illustration of Spiritual Richness

A country church I once served as a lay pastor reminds me
of one quality that Christ highlighted in His letter to the Smyrna
Church. This reminder of spiritual richness was particularly
notable during a Christmas program during my third year.

Advent, four weeks before Christmas, approached. The church
faced the annual dilemma of how to get enough people to put on the
Christmas pageant, for ours was a "small" church. About twenty
people attended each worship service on Sunday, and many of the
worshipers were senior citizens. Most of the members were limbs
on the same family tree.

I was happy that the lay pastor's job duties did not include
captaining the Christmas pageant.

One of the mothers in our church usually assumed this
responsibility. Each Christmas, this lady recruited the three
children who attended Sunday school and church (including
her own child). She dressed up the children in costumes, led in
the annual Christmas performance, led in the singing of a few
Christmas carols, and then turned everything over to Santa, who
appeared and handed out presents to the children.

This particular year, one of the returning former members
wanted to direct the Christmas pageant. She came to the session
(elders) meeting and presented plans for a big production, needing
many people.

The elders and I told her that her ideas sounded "great."
However, when she left the room, we all said, "We'll see." Bringing
her ideas into reality looked like a difficult project.

However, she started right away and recruited five men to
build the sets. To get men to do anything in this church often
constituted a miracle, but she got the men she needed, and all five
agreed to build the sets for the pageant.

Next, she started recruiting the characters needed.

She wanted a real baby Jesus. One of the members agreed to ask a local mother she knew to bring her baby to play the role.

She wanted four animal costumes (a cow, a donkey, and two sheep) and six people to fill them. Two church members agreed to make the costumes and volunteered to find four adult friends to join them as the cow and donkey in the stable and the sheep in the field.

She wanted four shepherds, seven angels, and three wise men. Two mothers of the three children agreed to have their girls in the pageant, and the mothers and their daughters volunteered to recruit all the other shepherds, angels, and wise men.

She asked me to be the innkeeper.

Much faster than any of us had expected, she recruited everyone she needed except for Mary and Joseph.

After church one Sunday morning three weeks before Christmas, a few folks brainstormed about possible people to play Mary and Joseph. Then one of the members stood up and said, "My daughter and her husband both get paroled from prison next week, and I would like to see both of them get involved in our church again."

"Do you think they could play the roles of Mary and Joseph?" the director asked.

Their mother agreed to ask them. After doing so, she then informed the director that they agreed to do the pageant roles of Mary and Joseph, but needed housing before they could make a commitment. After one of the members offered a vacant rental trailer that the couple could stay in until they got back on their feet, Mary and Joseph joined the cast of the pageant.

Rehearsal practices went well. I kept my eye on Mary and Joseph—and they kept theirs on me. Sometimes during rehearsals, they would come to the door of my inn, and just grin and stare at me until the director needed them. They confessed that being inside a church instead of a prison was taking some time to get used to.

When the Sunday night of the pageant arrived, one aware of its capacity would not believe that little church could be so filled. Counting the participants and the audience, there were almost one hundred people in attendance!

As the pageant began, Mary and Joseph walked slowly down the church aisle. Then, stepping up on the platform, they reached the inn. Joseph knocked several times before I responded and opened my door. He then asked me if there was any room, for he and his wife who would soon bear their child. After I regretfully told them that every room in the inn was filled, their expressions of regret were so lifelike. Then they quickly exited the church through a back door behind the set. At this point, the director-narrator read the Scripture about what happened after Mary and Joseph found no room in the inn, but were offered space in the stable behind it.

The two principal actors reentered the sanctuary in darkness. The spotlight then focused upon them as they stood at the manger scene on stage, at which a cow, to be expected in a stable, was present. As Mary tenderly held baby Jesus while Joseph looked on over her shoulder, you could feel the Spirit of the Lord in our midst. We all looked on in wonder.

Then the lights went off as a night star sky set replaced the stable set. As the director-narrator slowly read the narration for Luke 2:8–14, a spotlight illuminated the shepherds gathered with their sheep. Then another spotlight was switched on to illuminate the angel who appeared to the frightened shepherds in the night sky and told them, "Do not be afraid. I bring you good news of great joy that will be for all the people. Today in the town of David a Savior has been born to you; he is Christ the Lord. This will be a sign to you: You will find a baby wrapped in cloths and lying in a manger" (verses 10–12). Next, the rest of the angels joined him as the light beam widened to include all of them saying together to the shepherds, "Glory to God in the highest, and on earth peace to men on whom his favor rests" (verse 14).

After the spotlight went off, the angels went offstage and the shepherds spoke, "Let's go to Bethlehem and see this thing that has happened, which the Lord has told us about" (verse 15). With the lights out, the scenery reverted to the stable again, and the shepherds came down the aisle as the spotlight followed them to see baby Jesus, lying in a manger as His beaming earthly parents looked on. After seeing the Christ Child, the shepherds quickly left to share their good news, as the narrator read verse 17. The director then said, "Tonight you are seeing the true meaning of Christmas. The true meaning is the birth of Christ the Lord, the Savior who offers eternal life to all who will accept Him. Won't you share this good news to those who think Christmas is only about Santa Claus and special decorations and family meals?"

The final performance was for the wise men to come to worship baby Jesus and to bring Him their special gifts. Following the last presentation, all those who had a part in the pageant came on stage and, as their parts were called, they left the stage, accompanied with applause, hurrying down the aisle.

The director did an excellent job overseeing this pageant. The Christmas story came alive for all those in the audience that night. The sets were realistic and so were the people who played roles. Making clear the true meaning of Christmas as the birth of the Savior who offered salvation to all people, it was a "spiritually rich" performance.

In Isaiah, we read: "Once more the humble will rejoice in the LORD; the needy will rejoice in the Holy One of Israel" (Isa. 29:19).

Christianity embraces the poor, the downtrodden, the lonely, the weak, the mentally ill, the convict, the ex-con, and any other one rejected by the world. Yet, many professing Christians look down their noses at churches like the Smyrna Church, which are humble and poor in the eyes of the world. To refuse to attend such a church is to reject those whom Christ dearly loves.

Signs of a Smyrna Church

Do you know how to recognize churches like the one in Smyrna? All of these churches must be true to the Word of God. They must also be dynamic in consecration, worship, service, and witness. Their members must grow spiritually each day and need to be willing to suffer for the cause of Christ, no matter the consequences. These characteristics can be found in:

- Storefront churches

- Churches that conduct worship services in schools and civic centers

- Churches that conduct worship services in inexpensive, prefabricated buildings;

- Country churches that conduct worship services in rural settings

- Churches that have no prefatory titles of "mega" or "super"

- Any church of any size.

An Illustration of Christians Suffering Persecution

This illustration is from Dr. Lon Ackelson, co-author.

I was so excited when I received the call to my first church as a senior pastor. I was fresh out of seminary, having graduated one month before my wife and I moved to our new small community to begin this new ministry. Filled with great expectations, I decided to begin a campaign of visitation the day after we moved. I had no idea that when I introduced myself and told what church I pastored, most people would act as if they saw a shark fin heading their way in the ocean.

After smiling and introducing myself, I found out that just about none of these people wanted to get to know the new minister in town, and some slammed the door in my face as soon as they heard the name of my church! In fact, the name of my church seemed to leave a bad taste in the mouths of most of the people I visited.

After knocking on the doors of homes within two blocks of the church, I finally found an open door. The lady who stood in the doorway told me that she used to come to my church but stopped after learning that the church ladies circle was a weekly gossip session. She also told me that the church had split twice. I knew about the latest split (it occurred under the pastor who was my predecessor), but not until then about a theological split twenty years earlier.

Each week that I visited people in the community, I faced persecution because of bad experiences the people had in my church before my time. Sometimes the unpleasant experience was that of a relative or friend, but because of it, the person I visited refused to ever attend my church and they treated me as unwelcome in their home.

My enthusiasm to launch myself into the new community I served waned considerably as I encountered unexpected and unpleasant receptions in most of the homes in the neighborhood of the church. My church had a reputation that turned off many people in the community. The recent split involved a difference between the pastor and the board concerning his message topics. After the pastor said that *he* would decide what topics to preach, the board fired him. His current lengthy series had been on science and the Bible, and those tired of the series sought a different topic, but he refused to change.

He took about half of the church family (who sympathized with him) to begin a new church in a nearby school. At one home I visited, a lady asked me why she should go to a church where the people do not get along with each other. Another resident reported that people in a bar he frequented were better behaved than the people in my church were.

I expected a warm welcome, not persecution, from the people of my new community. I expected the same from my new congregation. However, about two months after my ministry began, an elder and his wife walked out of a midweek Bible study when they did not agree with my interpretation of Scripture. The elder declared loudly and angrily that I was wrong in the view I set forth, and when I did not agree, he and his wife left the service. As they walked home, their pastor silently asked God to open the earth under them and swallow them up.

Later I repented of my sin when those two angry members left the church service early, but I found one difficult problem after another during that initial year. By the end of my first year, I was ready to quit. However, my wife and I decided to visit several pastors we knew and seek their advice about our future. The result of these visits helped us in our future decision. We learned that the first pastorates of our pastor friends were often unexpectedly problem-ridden, and showed them the need to depend on the Lord for every need. They counseled us to take our problems to the Lord and grow spiritually because of our experiences.

Though I never faced persecution like those in the Smyrna Church did (from Jews and Romans who hated Christ and those who reminded them of Him), I still faced persecution when doors slammed and when I was verbally attacked, as a representative of a church that people hated. I may not have been harmed physically nor had my life threatened like those at Smyrna, but I was assaulted emotionally.

I learned to provide pastoral care when people of the community were hospitalized or bereaved. Over time, new people visited the church. As I was faithful to preach the Word and to live it, spiritual growth occurred within the congregation and the negative reputation of the church diminished—but some lingering bad feelings still provided excuses for several residents to stay away from our church.

Part II: How Jesus Encouraged Overcomers of the Church at Smyrna

Christ held the Smyrna Church up to His light and said, *"Be faithful, even to the point of death, and I will give you the crown of life"* (Rev. 2:10). Christ encouraged this church to be brave even if they heard their enemies sent by satan knocking at their door and not to fear any suffering for their faith. Smyrna meant "myrrh," which was symbolic of death. Smyrna's history has been one of successive sackings, fires, and destructions. Christ called for faithfulness to Him even if it meant death and promised the "crown of life" for all martyrs or those willing to take a stand for Christ even at the loss of their lives in Smyrna. The "crown of life" refers to a special dimension of eternal life for those who receive it. "Blessed is the man who perseveres under trial, because when he has stood the test, he will receive the crown of life that God has promised to those who love him" (Jas. 1:12). This reward in heaven is special to those who face persecution for their faith or become martyrs.

A church like the one at Smyrna has faithful members who are pilgrims here, where they experience the "abundant life," and home in heaven, where they will experience a special dimension of "eternal life" given to all who face persecution as believers. These churches are spiritually rich in consecration, worship, service, and witness for the Lord, and do not shirk opportunities to share the gospel, no matter the consequences.

Christ's light shines on such churches when they meet for worship.

Christ's light shines on such churches when they have an old-fashioned revival service.

Christ's light shines on such churches when they have a weekly prayer meeting.

Christ's light shines on such churches when they have a weekly home Bible study.

Christ's light shines on these church members when they walk with the Lord daily.

Christ's light shines on these church members when they are persecuted for being Christians.

Churches like the Smyrna Church are heavenly churches.

Even though trials and tribulations may befall the members of a church like the Smyrna Church during the week, the Holy Spirit helps them overcome every adversity by faith that is only strengthened through trials.

To each of these believers, Christ says, "Well done, my good servant!" (Luke 19:17).

Christ Doesn't Shine His Light on All Churches

If only all churches were as spiritually rich as the one in Smyrna. However, many churches align with the passage in Isaiah where the Lord said through the pen of the prophet Isaiah, "These people come near to me with their mouth and honor me with their lips, but their hearts are far from me. Their worship of me is made up only of rules taught by men" (Isa. 29:13). "These people" were the Jews of Jerusalem, whose religion had deteriorated to externals only in the time of Isaiah. They thought that God rewarded outward pious observances and rituals. Oh, if only they paid attention to the teaching and prophecy of Isaiah!

So many professing Christians are caught up in traditional churches and act like the Jews who said evil things against the Smyrna Church that Christ addressed. Why cannot those who profess Christianity display the same concern as the Smyrna Church believers for a spiritual life rich in consecration, worship, service, and witness? Why cannot professing Christians accept any cost in order to proclaim the gospel message? If your church is not like the one at Smyrna, may God help you to find one that is.

To all of you pastors and church leaders who bring a full spiritual life to your church, like the church at Smyrna, we thank God for you.

For all of you pastors and church leaders who look out on your congregation on Sunday morning and see the sleepy eyes of boredom, please ask God for the spiritual life that Christ gave to the church at Smyrna. It is available when we humble ourselves and yield to the lordship of Christ.

For all of you members of churches who are part of churches like the one at Smyrna, praise God!

If you see characteristics of the church at Smyrna wanting

in your church, ask God to lay it on the hearts of your spiritual leaders to bring those characteristics back.

> *"He who has an ear, let him hear what the Spirit says to the churches"* (Rev. 2:11).

Christ's Church needs to experience a rich spiritual life.

Suggestions for the Local Church

For the Christian, our spiritual life finds sustenance at church each Sunday morning or evening in the church worship service. To experience a rich spiritual life is to experience a rich time of worship each week on the Lord's Day. However…

The scenes for worship are changing.
The songs for worship are changing.
The words for worship are changing.

Tim Hughes and Soul Survivor

Tim Hughes, songwriter and worship leader for Soul Survivor, expresses a new standard of holiness in worship with these words from his song *Here I Am to Worship:*

Light of the world, You stepped down into darkness,
Opened my eyes, let me see beauty that made this heart
adore You.
Hope of a life spent with You,
King of all days, oh, so highly exalted,
Glorious in heaven above, humbly you came
To the earth, You created all for love's sake became poor.
I'll never know how much it cost to see my sin
upon that cross.
Here I am to worship;
Here I am to bow down;
Here I am to say that You're my God.
You're altogether lovely,
Altogether worthy,
Altogether wonderful to me.

In his book, *Here I Am to Worship,* Tim Hughes shares with the reader some of these new and holier standards for worship leadership in today's churches.

Here are some passages from *Here I Am to Worship:*

A Heart After God

Worship leaders must be constantly inquiring of the Lord. We need to be so desperate for God that we will do whatever it takes to follow Him. We will be so much more effective in our ministries if we seek the will of God and do it. This involves spending time with our heavenly Father. We cannot know the heart of God without first being still and listening. For each of us, the hidden place with God is critical. Sadly, we all too often let our ministries get in the way of our relationship with God. We become so busy that the noise of the world around us drowns out the voice of the Lord. We find ourselves more focused on doing the work of the Lord than seeking the Lord of the work.

If we are not learning how to worship before Him on our own, then how can we stand before others and lead them in worship?[1]

Seek Humility

In the context of worship, there is only one star, and that is Jesus. He alone is the famous One. As worship leaders, we need to be aware of pride taking root in our hearts. The truth is that pride is often a very subtle thing, but if not addressed, it can rule us. We have a responsibility to actively seek humility.[2]

Live Our Worship

We at Soul Survivor have been really challenged by this well-known phrase: "Preach the gospel at all times and if necessary use words." We need to proclaim the good news, but we also need to demonstrate it. With this in mind, we have organized outreaches into the local community where we serve by picking up litter, painting houses, and cleaning up people's gardens. It has been amazing to see all that God has done among people as we serve them in simple ways. We have discovered that social outreach is not just evangelistic, but it is also tied up with our worship. If we only proclaim our worship with our words and do not live out our worship by serving people with our lives, something is wrong. God says through the prophet Amos:

> *I hate, I despise your religious feasts; I cannot stand your assemblies. Even though you bring me burnt offerings and grain offerings, I will not accept them. Though you bring choice fellowship offerings, I will have no regard for them. Away with the noise of your songs! I will not listen to the music of your harps. But let justice roll on like a river, righteousness like a never-failing stream!* (5:21–24).

In this passage, God clearly says that if we do not live lives of justice and concern for others, He hates our worship.[3]

Authenticity

When David was about to square off with Goliath, King Saul told David to try on Saul's own armor. However, David was swimming in the king's fighting gear and instead opted for a sling and five stones—not much really when it comes to state-of-the-art fighting equipment. However, David was not going to pretend to be something he was not. He was going to be his own man... Sometimes it is very tempting to watch gifted worship leaders and crave what they have. Occasionally we even try to copy exactly what they do, hoping that as a result we will be more effective. This of course is nonsense. God has gifted us in unique and individual ways. Unfortunately, I will never have the guitar skills of Eric Clapton or the voice of Bono, but that does not matter, since God delights in using me the way I am—the way He created me to be.[4]

Respect for Leadership

Sadly, the relationship between pastor and worship leader is all too often one of conflict. So many misunderstandings and insecurities surround this partnership. While pastors usually are not blameless when the relationship breaks down, I primarily want to look at this issue from the perspective of a worship leader. God calls us to honor and respect those in leadership over us, even when that is sometimes very tough. Occasionally, pastors may be too controlling, they may not give enough space for singing worship, or they may not understand us. However, this never justifies a response of disobedience or divisiveness on our part.

The relationship between pastors and worship leaders has to work two ways. Out of this understanding, we choose to respect and defer to our leaders.[5]

Two Worship Manuals To Consider

Here I Am To Worship has excellent information about cutting-edge contemporary worship and how to integrate it in your church. Another worship book, *The Worship God Is Seeking,* is written by David Ruis, a well-known worship leader from Canada. This second book helps focus our worship, not as it pleases worshipers, but as it pleases and is centered on God. Both books are excellent additions to the library of every worship leader. Later in this chapter, you will learn how to acquire these two books.

David Ruis and the Worship God Seeks

Here are some key passages from *The Worship God Is Seeking*:

God is the Only Focus in Worship

The fact is that worship is an end in itself. It is for God. To lose sight of Him is to lose sight of worship altogether. All begins and ends with Him.

The stance is not passive, however. This kind of worship is engaged. Repeatedly in the book of Revelation, we see the elders throwing down their crowns, bowing low before their God (see Rev. 4:9–11). The original language is clear. It is voluntary. This is not reaction to being overwhelmed by His glory or overcome by something external. The elders are moved by the revelation of whom it is they stand before and, by a deliberate act of the will, they bow.

"You are worthy, our Lord and God, to receive glory and honor and power, for you created all things, and by your will they were created and have their being" (Rev. 4:11).

A Shift in Focus

The resulting power of this kind of worship shifts the focus from the worshippers to the One being worshipped. The attention shifts from the worship team, the choir, the liturgist, and the preacher to the Lord. No longer is worship about performance and presentation. God is present. This posture is deliberate, not waiting for a mystical presence but stepping into the reality of who God is. No longer is worship simply about receiving a touch and getting goose bumps. God is here, and His kingdom has come.

It is in this place that God reveals Himself as He chooses to descend and dwell with His Church. This is the biblical understanding of worship. Even though God dwells in the courts of heaven with angels and living creatures in attendance, He condescends to inhabit the praise of his people (see Ps. 22:3); Jesus is found in the midst of the congregation singing to the Father (see Heb. 2:12); and as we draw near to God, He draws near to us (see Jas. 4:8). The Holy Spirit, proceeding from the Father and the Son, has freedom here to glorify Christ, establishing righteousness, judgment, and justice, empowering the Church to do His work.

As God draws near, so the fullness of His Triune presence and His kingdom come. To invite God's presence is to invite His kingdom reign. All agendas must be laid aside for His. All other authorities and powers must submit to Him or face the consequences. There is no room for idols. All that is false will be exposed. The true worship experience is not a liturgy devoid of power and life-changing implications. The King is here, and His kingdom has come.

Worship That Challenges Comfort Levels

At times, we may be uncomfortable with this kind of worship encounter. The worship that focuses on God first, acknowledging His presence among us, can be unsettling. We are not welcoming a force to empower us, nor invoking the presence of a distant deity. This is not about aligning ourselves with good ideas or philosophizing about the concept of God. It is about acknowledging that He is real. He is alive. God has thoughts, opinions, feelings, and insight about what is happening among us. Just as we see Jesus strolling through the churches in Revelation, evaluating what He observed, so, too, He interacts with the Church today, wanting to be fully included in the life of our community and fellowship with us (see Rev. 3:20). Isn't this amazing!

Worship Is Personal

So then, making way for God in our worship is not something

vague or theoretical. What makes worship truly Christian is its proximity. God is in the room. Worship is now not only objective, it is also deeply personal. Songs are no longer just *about* God, they are sung *to* God. Displays of adoration are not inappropriate but are a vital part of the worship's authenticity. Worship becomes about responding to God's presence. The dynamics of the liturgy change from that of a monologue to a dialog and response as the present rule and reign of heaven break through. God is here, and we will never be the same.[6]

In *Here I Am to Worship* by Tim Hughes, and *The Worship God Is Seeking* by David Ruis, we see the words of John Henry Newman come alive about having a heavenly church on earth. In the worship ideals of these Christian worship leaders, help is offered to make church like heaven—a place where God the Father, God the Son, God the Holy Spirit, and the priesthood of believers gather together to worship.

Ruis' book offers insight on what worship should really be all about and how it should be implemented in a church program; and Hughes' book offers many practical tips and much good advice for leading worship, leading a praise band, choosing a song list, and musical dynamics. Both books are cutting-edge worship manuals for evangelical churches of the Twenty-First Century. Both books will help a worship leader who faces a difficult job convincing a pastor or board to transition from traditional to contemporary worship format.

You can order David Ruis' book, *The Worship God Is Seeking,* and Tim Hughes' book, *Here I Am to Worship,* in many local Christian bookstores. You can also order each book from Gospel Light at *www. gospellight.com* and enter a search for David Ruis or Tim Hughes (worship leaders are also referred here to a contemporary worship website of Tim Hughes where they can sign up for a free worship newsletter and download free worship songs to consider).

If you are a church member, this section of chapter two needs to be brought to the attention of whoever leads worship in your church. Tell this person that you've read some exciting information about contemporary worship that you would like to share with him. Then share these pages from chapter two with your worship leader.

3

True and False Pergamum Church
THE MESSAGE TO PERGAMUM

"To the angel of the church in Pergamum write:

"These are the words of him who has the sharp, double-edged sword. I know where you live—where Satan has his throne. Yet you remain true to my name. You did not renounce your faith in me, even in the days of Antipas, my faithful witness, who was put to death in your city—where Satan lives.

"Nevertheless, I have a few things against you: You have people there who hold to the teaching of Balaam, who taught Balak to entice the Israelites to sin by eating food sacrificed to idols and by committing sexual immorality. Likewise you also have those who hold to the teaching of the Nicolaitans. Repent therefore! Otherwise, I will soon come to you and will fight against them with the sword of my mouth.

"He who has an ear, let him hear what the Spirit says to the churches. To him who overcomes, I will give some of the hidden manna. I will also give him a white stone with a new name written on it, known only to him who receives it" (Rev. 2:12–17).

The Background of Pergamum

Pergamum, capital of Asia, was situated on a hill about 1000 feet high and commanded the fertile valley of the Caicus River in southern Mysia. The city stood opposite the island of Lesbos about eighteen miles from the Aegean Sea and communicated with the sea via the Caicus, which was navigable by small craft. Pergamum was also located on the great North-South road that ran from Ephesus to the city of Cyzicus on the Sea of Marmara.

The city's real history began in the third century B.C. under the Attalid dynasty, when it became the capital of a Greek kingdom of considerable importance. Attabus III willed his kingdom to Rome at his death in 133 B.C., when it became the province of Asia. The Greek Pergamene kings (so called because Pergamum held the castle of each king) owed their power to expand to their skillful management of the country's natural wealth, which they bestowed freely as patrons of the arts and made Pergamum one of the greatest and most beautiful Greek cities. It was laid out in terraces on a hillside. A city also developed at the foot of the hill; there was located a famous health resort dedicated to the pagan god Asclepius (Greek-Roman god of medicine, the son of Apollo). Pergamum was renowned for its school of sculpture.

Excavations of almost 130 years at the site of Pergamum have now uncovered some sixty percent of the ancient city. The great sculptured altar of Zeus there has been identified by some as "Satan's throne" (Rev. 2:13).

Part I: Jesus' Positive Evaluation of the Church at Pergamum

Notice that Jesus commends this church for two very good things they have done:

"I know (1) where you live [in the midst of satanic temptations to worship Roman emperors]. Yet you remain true to my name. (2) You did not renounce your faith in me [even when my faithful witness was martyred in your midst]" (Rev. 2:13). Antipas was the first martyr of Asia. According to tradition, he was slowly roasted to death in a bronze kettle during the reign of the Emperor Domitian.

Jesus said two positive things about the church at Pergamum. They were Christians (1) who took a stand for Christ and (2) did so even under the worst persecution imaginable. Pergamum was the official center of emperor worship in Asia, and thus intolerant to Christians who refused to do what all other Roman citizens added to their religious duties: worship the emperor as a god.

Part II: Jesus' Negative Evaluation of the Church at Pergamum

Although Jesus described two instances of commendable Christian conduct to describe the Christians in the Pergamum Church in one verse of Revelation 2, He devoted *two verses* to the two negative things He had to say about some in this church: toleration of two areas of false doctrine in the church: (1) sexual immorality and (2) idolatry. Notice, in verse 20, that these are the same two areas tolerated by the Thyatira Church.

Balaam advised the Midianite women how to lead the Israelites astray through immorality and idolatry (see Num. 25:1–2; 31:16; and Jude 1:11). Nicolaitans were a heretical sect within the church that had worked out a compromise with the pagan society around them. The teaching of Balaam allowed Christians to marry pagans, and the teaching of Nicolaitans asserted that since heathen gods did not exist anyway, Christian participation in idolatrous feasts couldn't hurt them. They apparently taught that spiritual liberty as Christians gave them sufficient leeway to practice idolatry and immorality. Tradition identifies them with Nicolas, the proselyte of

Antioch who was one of the first seven deacons in the Jerusalem church (Acts 6:5), though the evidence is merely circumstantial. There is no clear evidence that Nicolas later in life practiced pagan doctrines, but those who did this adopted his name.

Both the Pergamum Church and the Thyatira Church were charged by Christ with tolerating the same grievous sins: immorality and idolatry. In this book, chapter four will focus on the specific sins of immorality and idolatry taught by a false prophet named Jezebel. Christ devoted *four verses* to these issues when addressing the Thyatira Church and cited by name a false prophet on the church staff. Addressing the Pergamum Church, Christ said that He was against the Pergamum Church because some of their members had fallen away from Him and held the teachings of Balaam and the Nicolaitans. Those teachings happened to be that immorality and idolatry were okay for Christians because of their spiritual liberty. This was an example of allowing those who held false doctrine to infiltrate a church's membership and seek to draw away other members.

Go back to the beginning of this chapter and reread Revelation 2:12–17. You will read about two positive and two negative features of the Pergamum Church. Now take a brief period to answer the following four questions as they relate to the Pergamum Church. Finally, answer the fifth question about your local church. Check Y for yes, N for no, CD for cannot determine, and DK for do not know. (Check the answers under this exercise only after you have answered each question as best you can.)

1-Does the *worship* of members of the Pergamum Church please Christ?
__Y __N __CD __DK

2-Does the *work* of members of the Pergamum Church please Christ?
__Y __N __CD __DK

3-Does the *witness* of members of the Pergamum Church please Christ?
__Y __N __CD __DK

4-What about the Pergamum Church displeases Christ?

5-Which positives and/or negatives about the Pergamum Church are present in your local church?

(Answers: 1-CD [nothing is said about worship], 2-Y [implies good works] or CD [nothing is specifically said about work], 3-Y [implies witnessing for Christ under severe persecution] or CD [nothing is specifically said about witnessing], 4-Some members believe false doctrine: sexual immorality and idolatry are okay for Christians, 5-Answers will vary.)

Now, let's see how people in the Pergamum Church might answer the same questions for which you just filled out answers.

Dear members and leaders of the Church in Pergamum, what are your answers to the following three questions?

Does the *worship* of members of your church please Christ?

Does the *work* of members of your church please Christ?

Does the *witness* of members of your church please Christ?

Those who believed false doctrine would probably answer each question in the affirmative. They would likely label themselves as broad-minded Christians who enjoyed freedom in Christ.

Some members of this church, who were not members of false doctrine groups, would probably tell you to talk to their spiritual leaders to answer these questions.

Some of these professing Christians would be in a quandary how to answer the questions. They would not be sure about any of their answers or their beliefs.

The Pergamum Church seemed to have found the right path at one time in their early history; then, some people who held false doctrine began attending the church. "Those people" began to infiltrate the church and led many members astray.

We all probably remember a special class of "those people" from our teenage years. They were the kind who would give invitations like these:

- "Let's ask Benny to buy us some beer."

- "Let's go to Jane's house and see if she has any dope."

- "Let's all go to Doug's lake cabin tonight for skinny dipping and partying with no adults on board."

- "Let's skip classes today and see who can 'lift' the most merchandise from the corner store without getting caught."

You may remember "those people" in your youthful peer group; they are the ones who always promoted a life of sinful pleasures. You may or may not have given in to their suggestions, but you probably heard them during break times at your middle or high school. You know all about "those people," unless you led a very sheltered life as a youth.

Jesus told the congregation at Pergamum that they had "those people" right inside their church! These folks were professing Christians, but they believed false doctrines.

In chapters two and three of Revelation, Jesus told all the congregations He addressed (except the Smyrna Church and the Philadelphia Church) that they contained members who were faithful and true and those who were soiled and sinful, but the Church of Pergamum seemed to have more of the latter than the former.

In the eyes of God, we are all either lost sinners or sinners saved by the Savior. However, lost sinners can acknowledge and repent of their sins, then accept Jesus Christ as their personal Savior. Those members of the Pergamum Church, who had a form of godliness only, can become sinners saved by the Savior.

On the other hand, lost sinners can find fun and fellowship in the soiled and sinful lifestyle of the Pergamum Church, thinking of anything but redemption. They can become one of "those people," who proudly advertise their membership in a church like the one at Pergamum. Thus, they can remain in their sinful ways and think that repentance is only for little old ladies and weaklings.

The problem at Pergamum, and at many modern-day churches, surfaces when "those people" become active members of the congregation.

"Those people" create trouble by trying to get God's people to join them on the wrong path. They cause dissension and distort the church's mission as showing love to pagans by marrying them and embracing their lifestyles. They lead others down the wrong path in their church by showing how Christians can wink at sin, and then embrace it.

The spiritual leaders of the Pergamum Church didn't bring heaven into their church; instead, they brought the things of the world system of satan into it. The Nicolaitans that the church permitted to be members believed unrestrained indulgence in anything that causes one pleasure—a damnable lie of satan! Ditto, the satanic doctrine of Balaam that okayed Christian-pagan marriages.

"Those People" of the First Century

Jesus experienced "those people" firsthand when He told the crowd in Capernaum that He was "the Bread of Life" (John 6:35, 48). Jesus Christ experienced the ire of "those people" when He told them that He had "come down from heaven" (verses 38, 41).

Some of "those people"—Jesus' neighbors, who were religious Jews—started grumbling. They said, "Is this not Jesus, the son of Joseph, whose father and mother we know? How can He now say, 'I came down from heaven'?" (John 6:42).

Jesus' ministry had started to grow. He had healed the sick (John 5:1–9; 6:2), had walked on water, and had calmed the hearts of His anxious disciples (6:16–20). He had fed the five thousand with five small loaves of bread and two small fish (6:5–14). The Good News had spread throughout Galilee and Judea, and many people followed Him as the One who could overthrow the Roman rulers and restore Israel to Jewish rule. Few people followed Him as their personal Messiah-Savior.

However, Jesus had not performed His ministry without encountering a bunch of detractors. There were many of "those people" who did not want to believe in Him, except as one who would overthrow the Romans. They did not want to follow the teachings of Christianity. They enjoyed an outward form of religion and did not want anyone to tell them they were wrong. "Those people" did not want to eat the Bread of Life that came down from heaven because they saw no reason to since they practiced the ceremonial religion of Judaism. Accepting a new world of redemption and righteousness was not what these people had any desire to do.

We learn that on that day in Capernaum, "On hearing it, many of His disciples said, 'This is a hard teaching. Who can accept it?'

"Aware that His disciples were grumbling about this, Jesus said to them, 'Does this offend you? What if you see the Son of Man ascend to where he was before! The Spirit gives life; the flesh counts for nothing. The words I have spoken to you are spirit and they are life. Yet there are some of you who do not believe.' For Jesus had known from the beginning which of them did not believe and who would betray him. He went on to say, 'This is why I told you that no one can come to me unless the Father has enabled him.'

"From this time many of his disciples turned back and no longer followed him" (John 6:60–66).

Christ's *"sharp, double-edged sword"* (Rev. 2:12) for the church at Pergamum symbolized divine judgment (see Isa. 49:2; Heb. 4:12). It meant that the sin of false doctrine within this church was going to be judged by Christ. The only way to avoid this judgment was for earnest conviction and repentance of sin. Those who tolerated false doctrine in the church faced the wrath of the Lord's sword, who wanted this teaching cut out of the church!

Jesus waved His sharpened sword throughout the crowd at Capernaum. Some allowed His gospel message to penetrate their sinful hearts and convict them of sin and their need of repentance, but many of "those people" in the crowd deflected every attempt by Jesus to get inside their lives. "Those people" of the first century believed there was no penalty for their sins and they had no need of salvation.

"Those People" of Old Testament Times

Moses and Aaron faced similar problems with "those people" in the desert wanderings of the children of Israel. "Those people," who worshipped God, even went so far as to say, "If only we had died by the LORD's hand in Egypt! There we sat around pots of meat and ate all the food we wanted, but you have brought us out into this desert to starve this entire assembly to death" (Exod. 16:3).

Moses then told Aaron, "Say to the entire Israelite community, 'Come before the LORD, for he has heard your grumbling.' While Aaron was speaking to the whole Israelite community, they looked toward the desert, and there was the glory of the LORD appearing in the cloud (Exod. 16:9–10). (Please share John's personal revelation of this verse at *www.dazzlinglight.org*)

"The LORD said to Moses, 'I have heard the grumbling of the Israelites. Tell them, 'At twilight you will eat meat, and in the morning you will be filled with bread. Then you will know that I am the LORD your God'" (Exod. 16:11–12).

"The people of Israel called the bread manna" (Exod. 16:31). Moses told Aaron to put some manna in a jar and place the jar in the Lord's presence to be kept for their descendents.

"As the LORD commanded Moses, Aaron put the manna in

front of the Testimony, that it might be kept" (Exod. 16:34).

Even after being fed, "those people" continued to cause trouble for Moses and Aaron. For later in their journey, "those people" led God's people and their spiritual leader Aaron astray with "revelry" (wild sex parties) and the worship of a golden calf idol (see Exod. 32:4–6).

Moses had to divide the camp. "Then he said to them, 'Whoever is for the LORD, come to me.' And all the Levites rallied to him!

Then Moses said, "This is what the LORD, the God of Israel, says: 'Each man strap a sword to his side. Go back and forth through the camp from one end to the other, each killing his brother and friend and neighbor.' The Levites did as Moses commanded, and that day about three thousand of the people died" (Exod. 32:26–28).

Moses then went back up the mountain to plead for the people's forgiveness. "The LORD replied to Moses, 'Whoever has sinned against me I will blot out of my book. Now go, lead the people to the place I spoke of, and my angel will go before you. However, when the time comes for me to punish, I will punish them for their sin" (Exod. 32:33–34).

God Reminds Us of What We Forget

We sometimes forget that God takes sin very seriously. We need a wake-up call like the words of God just quoted.

We sometimes forget that the work of Christ's Church represents the most important activity on earth: "The Spirit gives life; the flesh counts for nothing" (John 6:63).

We sometimes forget that satan will use any means and any individual to defeat Christ's congregations: "Satan himself masquerades as an angel of light. It is not surprising, then, if his servants masquerade as servants of righteousness" (2 Cor. 11:14–15).

Part III: Jesus' Corrective Command to the Church at Pergamum

Christ warns this church at Pergamum that they are right at satan's throne. Pergamum was the center of emperor worship in the Roman Empire—a worship sanctioned by satan. When Christians refused to worship the emperor, a duty for all citizens of the Roman Empire, they incurred persecution from people who considered them refusing to accept duties accepted by all Roman citizens, no matter their religion.

"Those people" in the church were willing to worship the emperor as well as Christ, compromising in order to be accepted by everyone. Those who served the interests of satan worked hard to get this church to follow false teaching. Christ commands this church: *"Repent!"* (Rev. 2:16). They needed to admit they were sinning and turn from their sinful behavior to Christ. To refuse to repent is to accept a losing fight with Christ's sharpened sword of judgment and premature death.

At the time of this letter from Christ, false teaching required physical circumcision for salvation and giving Christians the green light for sexual immorality, idolatry, emperor worship, and any other sins popular in the Roman Empire.

False Teaching in Today's Church

What are the false teachings "those people" are promoting in the church today? The Bible describes false teaching as any lifestyle that promotes conformity to "the pattern of this world [system of satan]" (Rom. 12:2). False teaching promotes a lifestyle that looks for the easy (usually also satan's) way out. Such teaching promotes a lifestyle of escapism to the allurements provided by satan.

In the churches of today, this false teaching appears in these ways:

- Promotions that encourage living to satisfy self-desires.

- Plans that offer heightened levels of personal fulfillment.

- Schemes that promise financial gain because of an active faith.

- Teachings that are popular but compromise Bible doctrine.

One way to determine what is false teaching is to note what is opposite each teaching:

- Living to satisfy self-desires is the opposite of living to satisfy what Christ desires.

- Personal fulfillment is the opposite of personal sacrifice.

- Financial gain is the opposite of spiritual gain.

- Compromised doctrine is the opposite of pure, true doctrine.

I sang the first two verses of the hymn, *Eternal God, Whose Power Upholds*, at Amity Presbyterian Church (see chapter seven for the setting). One powerful stanza was: "Help us to spread thy gracious reign till greed and hate shall cease and kindness dwell in human hearts, and all the earth find peace." The pastor told me that it was as if Jesus Himself sang through my lips, giving the most emphatic tone on the words, "Till greed and hate shall cease." This message from Christ reminded me that greed and hate consume many of today's churches. As examples, we need only look to the vast fortune of the Catholic Church and the Mormon Church, and the many Protestant churches that represent the last bastions of racism.

How do we deal with "those people" in our church, who are trying to lead God's people away from the cause of Christ into false doctrine? We must be bold and ask them the biblical basis for their belief. When such a basis is wanting, they need to acknowledge that they are sinning and that they need to repent of their sins! Have them read Revelation 2:12 and realize that Christ will cut them out of His Church if they do not repent of their sins.

Part IV: How Jesus' Encouraged Overcomers of the Church at Pergamum

If the members and leaders can purge themselves of false teaching and repent of their sin, then Christ made this promise: *"To him who overcomes, I will give some of the hidden manna* [heavenly food in contrast to the unclean food of the Balaamites]. *I will also give him a white stone with a new name written on it, known only to him who receives it* [an admission ticket to a heavenly banquet with the name of the spiritual overcomer on it]" (Rev. 2:17). This is a picture of the blessings awaiting believers in heaven. However, "those people," who do not repent of their sin and are never saved spiritually—though they call themselves Christians—will face the consequences of their sin: spiritual death.

If you have a problem with false teaching at your church, you should address it now, so that when Christ comes He will not have to say that it is necessary for Him to *"fight against them with the sword of my mouth"* (Rev. 2:16). He offers salvation, but those who reject His terms as their Savior accept Christ as their Judge.

Christ said that, if those tolerating or practicing false doctrine in the Pergamum Church refused to acknowledge and repent of their grievous sin, then they would face the consequences of drawing others in the church to sin, and He would fight them with His doubled-edged sword: the Word of Truth. They felt that the Word of God gave them freedom to practice immorality and idolatry. In reality, the word of satan gave them this false freedom.

What did this mean to those tolerating or practicing false doctrine in the Pergamum Church, who continued to live and refused to acknowledge that they were in sin? They would face a spiritual fight against Christ. If His sword did not cut into their hearts, it may well cut into their bodies. The Apostle Paul talked about something like this when he warned the Christians in Corinth about empty worship: "For anyone who eats and drinks without recognizing the body of the Lord eats and drinks judgment on himself. That is why many among you are weak and sick, and a number of you have fallen asleep" (1 Cor. 11:29–30). Christ's sword is a warning to bring conviction of sin to hearts, but it also cuts to bring sickness and death when professing Christians persist in sinning.

> **"He who has an ear, let him hear what the Spirit says to the churches"** (Rev. 2:17).

Christ's Church needs to become vigilant in fighting against false teaching.

Suggestions for the Local Church

How do we fight against false teaching in our church?

How do we help our congregation lead a faithful and true lifestyle so they can avoid "those people" who try to lead us astray?

The answer to these questions is to offer your congregation the opportunity to grow spiritually through a better understanding of the fundamental doctrines of Christianity.

Banks train tellers to recognize counterfeit bills by showing them everything they can about genuine currency so they can detect any departure from the genuine as spurious. In the same manner, churches need to show Christians everything they can about the true doctrine of God so they can recognize any departure from the genuine as false doctrine.

Dr. Paul E. Little, one of the leading American writers and speakers in the 1960s and 1970s on the subject of how to tell others about Christ, taught not only evangelism but also the fundamentals of the Christian faith that every believer should know. He was a staff member of InterVarsity Christian Fellowship for a number of years, and reached many college and university students for Christ. Little wrote *How to Give Away Your Faith,* the notes of an evangelistic lecture series he gave at Wheaton College in 1963. Soon to follow were the books of the fundamentals of the Christian faith: *Know What You Believe* and *Know Why You Believe.* Later came *Know Who You Believe.*

Paul Little's book, *Know What You Believe* affords your church an excellent resource that will help everyone become grounded in the fundamentals of Christian doctrine. This doctrinal resource is for new believers, students, longtime Christians, small-group Bible study classes, and pastors or anyone on the church's ministry staff. When we know the truth of God's Word, we can instantly recognize any variation from the fundamentals of the Bible as false teaching we need to avoid.

After your church studies *Know What You Believe,* the main doctrinal resource, then you will want to study *Know Who You Believe* and *Know Why You Believe.* These books offer more doctrinal resources for a believer to understand the biblical identification of the God he or she worships: the doctrine of theology *(Know Who You Believe)* and the biblical basis for all of our beliefs as Christians: the doctrine of apologetics *(Know Why You Believe).*

Billy Graham wrote in the forward of *Know Who You Believe* that "in his unique way Paul describes 'the electricity of Christ's claim,' that He is the solution to the 'moral power failure' of our time. Then he shows how Jesus Christ speaks to us today as clearly as He did to the thief on the cross: 'You, too, can be with me in paradise.'"

Here are some excerpts from Paul Little's *Know What You Believe* that give you a taste of the rich spiritual meals you will find in this book about the fundamental doctrines of the Christian faith.

The Bible Is Inspired!

The Bible originated in the mind of God, not in the mind of man. It was given to man by *inspiration.* The Bible is not inspired as we say the writings of Shakespeare were inspired or the music of Bach was inspired. The biblical sense of inspiration means: *God so superintended the writers of Scripture that they wrote what He wanted them to write, disclosing the exact truth He wanted conveyed.*

The word *inspired* literally means "out breathed" (from the mouth of God). Timothy is not ambiguous; the words did not come from the writers themselves! Inspiration applies to the end result— the Scripture itself—a faulty script would be useless.[1]

A Perfect Man with a Mission

All of Scripture comes to life in the person of Jesus Christ. Christ was the perfect man. As such, He was without sin in thought, word, or deed. He was able to challenge His enemies with the question, "Can any of you prove me guilty of sin?" (John 8:46). His foes had no reply. He was totally obedient to the Father. He said, "My food…is to do the will of him who sent me to finish his work" (John 4:34).

Jesus Christ was, par excellence, "a man with a mission." He knew what was ahead for Him. He frequently said, at a point of crisis, "My time has *not yet* come" (John 2:4, italics added; see also John 7:6). Finally, He said, "The hour *has come* for the Son of Man to be glorified" (John 12:23, italics added). A little later, as He contemplated the awfulness of the cross, He said, "Now My heart is troubled, and what shall I say? 'Father, save me from this hour'?" (John 12:27). The reason He had come, as He had said, was to "seek and to save what was lost" (Luke 19:10) and to "give his life as a ransom for many" (Mark 10:45). So central is the death of Christ to an understanding of Christianity that we will [need to] discuss it more fully. [See this section of his book.][2]

Objections of Skeptics Are Answered

There have always been some objections to the substitutionary death of Christ. Is not God all-powerful? Is not God all-living and able to pardon sin without requiring sacrifice? "Why can't He simply forgive sin out of His pure mercy?" skeptics want to know. "Could not an all-powerful God, in His omnipotence, have redeemed the world as easily as He created it? Since God commands man to forgive freely, why does He Himself not freely forgive?"

This logical question came to Archbishop Anselm in the

Twelfth Century, who crystallized the biblical teaching, focusing on forgiveness from God's viewpoint: "God's will is not His own in the sense that everything is permissible to Him or becomes right because He wills it...God cannot deal with sin except as in His holiness He perceives it. If He did not punish it, or make adequate satisfaction for it, then He would be forgiving it unjustly" (R.A. Finlayson, *The Story of Theology.* Downers Grove, Ill.: Intervarsity Press, 1963, p. 381).[3]

The Problem of Total Depravity

Some skeptics today speak about man as "evolving" from a primitive condition, but the Bible (Rom. 1:18–32) sadly portrays his *descent* rather than *ascent.* The result has been given the theological term "total depravity." This expression of man's condition after the Fall has been widely misunderstood, with the result that the Christian position regarding man's sinful nature has sometimes been unjustly caricatured.

Man's total depravity affects *every area of his life*—he is blighted, but not everything about him is *totally bad.* His depravity is total in that without God's grace he would be forever lost and apart from God.

The tragedy of the Fall went far beyond Adam and Eve. It was race-wide in its effect: "Therefore, just as sin entered the world through one man, and death through sin, and in this way death came to all men, because all sinned" (Rom. 5:12).[4]

The Holy Spirit Is Our Best Counselor and Teacher

Through our salvation in Jesus Christ, we are rescued from death and depravity for a new and better way of life. For Jesus proclaimed that "the Counselor, the Holy Spirit, whom the Father will send in my name, will teach you all things and will remind you of everything I have said to you" (John 14:26).

The Holy Spirit is not only a person—He is deity. The Apostle Paul said, "Now the Lord is the Spirit" (2 Cor. 3:17). And again, "Don't you know that you yourselves are God's temple and that God's Spirit lives in you?" (1 Cor. 3:16). At the gathering of the Council of Jerusalem the disciples declared, "It seemed good to the Holy Spirit and to us..." (Acts 15:28).[5]

Membership Requirements of the Family of God

At the coming of the Holy Spirit on Pentecost, Christ's Church was born. Moreover, through Christ's Church, God has opened to the world a heavenly path. Paul Little helps us identify this path when he reminds us that in this first congregation, "requirements for church membership focused on the basics":

1. *Belief in the Lord Jesus Christ* was the first ingredient (Acts 2:38). Faith in Christ, which always includes repentance for sin, was and is the spiritual prerequisite to new life and membership in the body of Christ. When people asked Jesus the question, "What must we do to do the works God requires?" He answered, "The work of God is this: to believe in the one he has sent" (John 6:28–29).

2. *Baptism,* with repentance, was for everyone, "in the name of Jesus Christ for the forgiveness of your sins" (Acts 2:38). Then believers received the promised follow-up of "the gift of the Holy Spirit." In the early church, Jewish converts were baptized immediately. Repentance (repenting of sin that led to faith in Christ as one's Messiah [Savior]) and being publicly baptized were practically simultaneous. Faith brings

salvation which baptism authenticates. From the examples of the Apostle John, Jesus, Philip, and the Ethiopian, water baptism is the practice of those who believe in Christ as Savior. [Little also notes a belief about baptism that he does not hold]: Some earnest Christians believe that the "one baptism" (Eph. 4:5) is the baptism of the Holy Spirit, and that water baptism is not God's purpose for Christians today.

3. *Acting on revealed truth* was another membership requirement. Paul warned of false teachers arising within the church (Phil. 3:2), and Peter echoed the solemn theme (2 Pet. 2:1). Throughout the New Testament, there is emphasis on doctrinal purity and holiness of life. Doctrinal or moral impurity was to be purged from the church (1 Cor. 5:7).

4. *Witnessing* was a visible characteristic of the church as a whole. Some had the special gift of evangelism. Their goal was the communication and preservation of the Gospel message to the immediate world and throughout the entire world (Matt. 28:19–20; Acts 1:8).

5. *Serving* stood out as the normal function of church members as they met the physical and spiritual needs of both believers and unbelievers: "As we have opportunity, let us do good to all people, especially to those who belong to the family of believers" (Gal. 6:10). Christ Himself was the example; He "went around doing good" (Acts 10:38).[6]

Live As the People of God's Light

The Apostle Paul wrote to the church at Ephesus: "Be imitators of God, therefore, as dearly loved children and live a life of love, just as Christ loved us and gave Himself up for us as a fragrant offering and sacrifice to God.

"But among you there must not be even a hint of sexual immorality, or of any kind of impurity, or of greed, because these are improper for God's holy people. Nor should there be obscenity, foolish talk or coarse joking, which are out of place, but rather thanksgiving. For of this you can be sure: No immoral, impure or greedy person — such a man is an idolater — has any inheritance in the kingdom of Christ and of God. Let no one deceive you with empty words, for because of such things God's wrath comes on those who are disobedient. Therefore do not be partners with them.

"For you were once darkness, but now you are **light** in the Lord. Live as children of **light.** (for the fruit of the **light** consists in all goodness, righteousness and truth) and find out what pleases the Lord. Have nothing to do with the fruitless deeds of darkness, but rather expose them" (Eph. 5:1–11).

To help your congregation live in the light of Christ's glory and to help your church fight against false teaching, you can order Paul E. Little's books, *Know What You Believe, Know Who You Believe,* and *Know Why You Believe* from many Christian bookstores. Use *Know What You Believe,* which presents all the basic doctrines of the Word of God, before using the other two books. You can also order these books from *www.cookministries.com* or *www.amazon. com* by entering a search for Paul Little or the title of his book.

If you are a church member, do the same with this section of chapter three that was recommended for chapter two. Offer the opportunity to your pastor or small-group director to read these exciting pages for study materials that cannot help but profit any church. Small groups in the church can use these books as study guides to help each member of your church learn the Christian ABCs.

4

Tolerant Thyatira Church
THE MESSAGE TO THYATIRA

"To the angel of the church in Thyatira write:

"These are the words of the Son of God, whose eyes are like blazing fire and whose feet are like burnished bronze. I know your deeds, your love and faith, your service and perseverance, and that you are now doing more than you did at first.

"Nevertheless, I have this against you: You tolerate that woman Jezebel, who calls herself a prophetess. By her teaching she misleads my servants into sexual immorality and the eating of food sacrificed to idols. I have given her time to repent of her immorality, but she is unwilling. So I will cast her on a bed of suffering, and I will make those who commit adultery with her suffer intensely, unless they repent of her ways. I will strike her children dead. Then all the churches will know that I am he who searches hearts and minds, and I will repay each of you according to your deeds. Now I say to the rest of you in Thyatira, to you who do not hold to her teaching and have not learned Satan's so-called deep secrets (I will not impose any other burden on you): Only hold on to what you have until I come.

"To him who overcomes and does my will to the end, I will give authority over the nations—He will rule them with an iron scepter; he will dash them to pieces like pottery'—just as I have received authority from my Father. I will also give him the morning star. He who has an ear, let him hear what the Spirit says to the churches" (Rev. 2:18–29).

The Background of Thyatira

Thyatira was located fifty-two miles northeast of Smyrna on a main road joining the Caicus and Hermus river valleys. A great trading city, its height came about A.D. 100. There is evidence of more trade guilds there than in any other Asian city.

Lydia a seller of purple from Thyatira probably represented her guild at Philippi (Acts 16:14). The purple she sold was probably made in the region of Thyatira, which produced the well-known Turkey red, obtained from the madder root. Perhaps the city was evangelized from Ephesus. Christ through the pen of John addressed the church there (Rev. 2:18–29), scoring it for too much conformity to the pagan customs and practices of the day.

Part I: Jesus' Positive Evaluation of the Church at Thyatira

Notice that Jesus commends this church for six very good things they have done:

I know (1) your deeds, (2) your love and (3) faith, (4) your service and (5) perseverance, and (6) that you are now doing more than you did at first.

Jesus had six positive things to say about the church at Thyatira. They were professing Christians who (1) did good works, (2) demonstrated love (3) lived by faith or demonstrated their faith, (4) served others who had needs and had servant-hearts, (5) learned to react with perseverance (patience under extended trials) when persecuted as Christians, and (6) were doing more now (of items 1–5) than they did at first.

Part II: Jesus' Negative Evaluation of the Church at Thyatira

Although Jesus had described six instances of commendable Christian conduct to describe the Christians in the Thyatira Church in one verse of Revelation 2, He devoted *four verses* to the two negative things He had to say about this church: toleration of two areas of false teachings in the church: (1) sexual immorality and (2) idolatry.

The first teaching is exemplified today in several ways:

1. When churches approve gay pastors and same-sex teaching by those in authority.

2. When churches tolerate sexual immorality by doing nothing to fight the huge pornography businesses in their cities and everywhere on the Internet, and doing nothing to combat the powerful gay forces that want children and teens to learn in public schools that same-sex people are as normal as heterosexuals.

3. When churches wink at sexual immorality among their members, considering religious and physical lives separate entities.

4. When spiritual leaders of churches are addicted to porn sites, or when any member of the church is so addicted.

5. When parents of children and teenagers neglect to provide filters for porn sites in computers used by their children and teens.

6. When parents of children and teenagers neglect to place computers with Internet connections in a public location in the home and instead allow kids to be unsupervised when on the Web.

The second teaching is demonstrated:

1. When today's church members choose to watch a television show or movie, play a computer game, or allow other modern-day idols to occupy their time rather than going to a church or Sunday school meetings or small-groups where they will be fed spiritually.

2. When anything a Christian owns becomes more important than Christ in the believer's life (example: wealth is used exclusively for personal enrichment— not to reach others for Christ).

Immorality and Idolatry

Jesus' verdict for those in the church at Thyatira was that, no matter how many of the members and leaders had been living fine Christian lives outwardly, they had one big sinful defect that led to two huge sins:

> *"You tolerate that woman Jezebel, who calls herself a prophetess. By her teaching she misleads my servants into sexual immorality and the eating of food sacrificed to idols"* (Rev. 2:20).

Many of these professing Christians tolerated an angel in disguise who claimed to represent God and who taught that it was okay to be a Christian and live just like the people of the world. Since the world of the Roman Empire endorsed sexual immorality and idolatry, this false teacher likely said that these church members needed to live like non-Christians to reach them for Christ. We know from what Christ says in His letter to this church that Jezebel was a false Christian teacher and what she taught was what her true master, satan, wanted her to teach: to attract Christians to a sin (sexual immorality) that had a tiny DESTRUCTION OF YOUR LIFE price tag concealed and to another sin (idolatry) that had the same price tag secreted.

We also know from what Christ says in verse twenty-four to this church that Jezebel was highly versed in Gnosticism, which made distinctions between the body and the soul. Only the soul was to know God better. The body was considered sinful and only through practicing sin did Gnostics believe they could penetrate satan's seat and overcome his power over them. This belief was labeled "the dark secrets of satan." In reality, they believed a lie of satan as the truth. Only Christ could give the power to overcome the power of satan.

Notice that Christ first gave Jezebel the opportunity to repent of her sin before getting her attention with a big switch (Rev. 2:21). He also gave all Christians in Thyatira a similar opportunity by reading this letter to their church. Those who did not take this period to repent of their sin would face the consequences of their decision.

Go back to the beginning of this chapter and reread
Revelation 2:18–29. You will read about the six positive
and two negative features of the Thyatira Church. Now
take a brief period to answer the following four questions
as they relate to the Thyatira Church. Finally, answer the
fifth question about your local church. Check Y for yes, N
for no, CD for cannot determine, and DK for do not know.
(Check the answers under this exercise only after you
have answered each question as best you can.)

**1-Does the *worship* of members of the
Thyatira Church please Christ?
__Y __N __CD __DK
2-Does the *work* of members of the
Thyatira Church please Christ?
__Y __N __CD __DK
3-Does the *witness* of members of the
Thyatira Church please Christ?
__Y __N __CD __DK
4-What about the Thyatira Church
displeases Christ?**

**5-Which positives and/or negatives about the
Thyatira Church are present in your local church?**

(Answers: 1-CD [nothing is said about worship], 2-
Y [deeds and service], 3-CD [nothing is said about
witnessing] or Y ["service" may include witnessing],
4-They tolerate the teaching of sexual immorality and
idolatry, 5-Answers will vary.)

Part III: Jesus' Corrective Command to the Church at Thyatira

After informing the church in Thyatira of the behavior that offended Him, Christ said,

> *"I have given her time to repent of her immorality, but she is unwilling. So I will cast her on a bed of suffering, and I will make those who commit adultery with her suffer intensely, unless they repent of her ways. I will strike her children dead. Then all the churches will know that I am he who searches hearts and minds, and I will repay each of you according to your deeds"* (Rev. 2:21–23).

What were the consequences for the false teacher who promoted immorality and for those in the church who followed her? Christ told the false teacher who held forth in the Thyatira Church that she would be cast into a bed with others with whom she committed adultery. All of these people were *spiritual* adulterers, who mixed Christianity with the paganism of the Greco-Roman mindset of the first century. "Jezebel" was a false teacher, and so were her fellow-adulterers. They were all "spiritual" leaders who influenced professing Christians in Thyatira to tolerate sexual immorality because that was considered one doorway into satan's power room (a major delusion of those who believed it).

All of these spiritual adulterers would suffer terribly (in terms of eternal consequences to their souls). Christ also indicated that those in the church who followed Jezebel's false amoral teaching would be killed (by the enemies of Christians in Thyatira or otherwise die prematurely [see the warning against practicing sin of Christians in 1 Cor. 11:30]).

However, Jezebel was guilty of more than spiritual adultery.

She also taught her students to commit sexual immorality in order to overcome the power of satan—a huge lie of the deceiver that Christ correctly labels *Satan's so-called deep secrets* (Rev. 2:24)!

How does this consequence relate to today's immoral spiritual teachers and their church followers? Those who attack the temples of the Lord (physical bodies) of whatever time and in whatever manner reap terrible suffering. Those in the churches of today who follow false immoral teaching can still expect to be killed by God (their lives will end prematurely). Should spiritual adultery be the practice of believers today, the warning of 1 Corinthians 11:30 is still God's response to His children who demonstrate false advertising of the family of God.

Consequences of Tolerating Idolatry

Let's examine what Christ said in His letter that deals with the second sin He mentioned that Jezebel taught Christians. After informing the church in Thyatira of the behavior that offended Him, Christ said, *"I have given her time to repent of her immorality, but she is unwilling* [no implication that she *was* willing to turn from teaching immorality, but that she was unwilling to turn from her true master, satan, who made immorality very appealing to her and her students].

> *So I will cast her on a bed of suffering, and I will make those who commit adultery* [this is the marriage of paganism and Christianity exemplified by sexual immorality and idolatry] *with her suffer intensely, unless they repent of her ways* [spiritual adultery, sexual immorality, and idolatry]. *I will strike her children dead. Then all the churches will know that I am he who searches hearts and minds, and I will repay each of you according to your deeds"* (Rev. 2:20–23).

What are the consequences of the marriage of paganism and Christianity exemplified by idolatry? Idolatry has been a sin that has always been frowned on by God (see Exod. 20:3–5). The penalty that Christ gives for Jezebel's teaching of sexual immorality is the same for her false teaching of idolatry. Those who dabble in either sin are playing with fire. Christians who practice either or both sins can expect a premature death if they do not repent and confess their sins. For, the tempter in both cases is satan and since he cannot get the souls of Christians, he will do his best to destroy their bodies—of course, keeping the true price tag of these sins hidden in an attractively wrapped gift.

Part IV: How Jesus Encouraged Overcomers of the Church at Thyatira

Notice that not every member of the church at Thyatira was entangled in the false teachings of Jezebel:

"Now I say to the rest of you in Thyatira, to you who do not hold to her teaching and have not learned Satan's so-called deep secrets (I will not impose any other burden on you): Only hold on to what you have until I come. To him who overcomes and does my will to the end, I will give authority over the nations--He will rule them with an iron scepter; he will dash them to pieces like pottery'-- just as I have received authority from my Father. I will also give him the morning star" (Rev. 2:24–28).

Godly members of the church were informed by Christ that He would add no further burden to them (taking a stand for Christ in this church was a burden for devoted Christians). These believers sought from within to influence their church that had strayed theologically and biblically. Their church featured false spiritual teaching and Gnostic teachings, which Christ branded *Satan's so-called deep secrets*. Gnosticism taught that in order to defeat satan, one had to enter his stronghold, i.e., experience evil deeply. Sexual immorality and idolatry were thus considered doorways to satan's seat of power.

Believers in Thyatira who stayed in their church remind us of the members of liberal denominations today who choose to stay in their straying denominations, trusting that they can be part of a voting block to influence their bodies to return to their conservative roots.

> *"Only hold on to what you have until I come* [your godly lives as Christians]. *To him who overcomes* [satan is going to oppose you and try to entangle you in the false teaching of your church; you will be involved in a battle with satan as long as you live], *and does my will* [God's will, not that of self] *to the end, I will give authority over the nations—'He will rule them with an iron scepter; he will dash them to pieces like pottery'—just as I have received authority from my Father. I will also give him the morning star"* (Rev. 2:24–28).

Those who win the victory in spiritual warfare will be co-rulers with Christ over the nations of the world during the millennial reign of Christ on earth. They will serve as rulers who reward the obedient and faithful and discipline with an "iron rod" the disobedient and unfaithful. The "morning star" is an illustration of Christ's absolute rule, which He will share with Christians during the millennium.

Attempts of Presbyterians to Ordain Homosexual Pastors

The elders of the church I served as an interim pastor agreed to have a student from Union Theological Seminary preach at our church in 2004. I met his bus and we started to my house where he was to stay for the weekend.

Not long after the seminary student began his ride, he asked me what I thought about the Presbyterian Church ordaining homosexuals.

I replied that this practice was wrong in both my eyes and those of God.

He told me that the upcoming 2004 General Assembly vote to ordain homosexuals would fail by a narrow margin (the proposal actually failed by four votes).

He then said that at the next General Assembly in 2006, the same proposal would pass.

I asked him how he knew this.

He told me that there was a large group of homosexual women at his seminary and of both sexes in Presbyterian churches who were pushing this proposal, and no one was fighting against them.

I asked him why he thought that this bill would pass two years from now, but not in 2004.

He shared an incredible story: the Moderator of the General Assembly spoke at his seminary recently, and she assured the women there that their voice would be heard in the General Assembly, and they would not stop fighting until the proposal to ordain homosexuals had won the day in the Presbyterian Church.

When the student looked at me, he couldn't have missed how astounded I was.

After we reached home and I assisted my passenger with his

luggage, I called a local Presbyterian minister and asked if he knew anything of this pro-gay movement within our denomination.

He said that he had not heard anything like this, but that it did possibly explain something that had bothered him. He said that of the thirty-nine recent graduates from Union Theological Seminary, only nine applied for ordination. He now wondered if some of the others might be waiting for the motion to pass, so they would not have to lie about their sexual preferences on job applications.

Two years ago, I felt that if what the seminary student said was true, I hoped someone in the Presbyterian Church would bring the pro-gay people into the light of God's truth and let Jesus Christ reveal the darkness of their plans.

At the 2006 Presbyterian Assembly, a vote was held to retain the Book of Order's keeping "fidelity and chastity" in the ordination standard and marriage between only man and woman for candidates. However, the same motion gave leeway in applying the church's ordination standards to churches—in other words, ordination of same-sex candidates was fine if a church wanted leeway in the current ordination standard. The vote for this was 298–221, a 77 vote margin in favor of it.

The seminary student was wrong about changing the ordination standards in the Presbyterian Book of Order. The assembly voted down the motion to strike the current ordination standards by 234–287, a 53-vote margin against it. The same measure lost by four votes in 2004. Nonetheless, the 2006 assembly gave churches the opportunity to approve homosexual candidates. The student was right about homosexuals gaining a win in the ordination standards (should a church decide to make the standards subjective and thus reject them), but he was wrong about the motion to completely strike out the current standards.

"Nevertheless, I have this against you: You tolerate that woman Jezebel, who calls herself a prophetess. By her teaching she misleads my servants into sexual immorality ..." (Rev. 2:20).

"He who has an ear, let him hear what the Spirit says to the churches" (Rev. 2:29).

Christ's churches must not tolerate sexual sin or idolatry.

Suggestions for the Local Church

"Christian" means "Christ-like." This means that those who profess this title do the very things that Christ would do. Well, how do we know what Jesus would do?

We must study the gospels to learn the life and ministry of Christ if we are going to find out what Christ would do in the situations of life we confront. However, we don't find Christ facing immorality like we find in today's amoral society. The Jewish society of the first century was not amoral and on the contrary maintained moral principles of life. Thus we must use the wisdom God gives us through His Word to enlist additional resources to help our families, our congregations, and us avoid satan's sinful path of sexual immorality.

One such organization to help in the fight against this sin is the American Family Association. Founded in 1977 by Don Wildmon, the American Family Association represents and stands for traditional family values. At their website, *www.afa.net*, they disclose their objectives with the following statements:

Mission Statement

The American Family Association exists to motivate and equip citizens to change the culture to reflect biblical truth.

Philosophical Statement

The American Family Association believes that God has communicated absolute truth to man through the Bible, and that all men everywhere at all times are subject to the authority of God's Word. Therefore, a culture based on biblical truth best serves the well being of our country, in accordance with the vision of our founding fathers.

Battlefields in the Culture War

The American Family Association recognizes that our culture fights against…

Preservation of the Marriage and Family
Decency and Morality
Sanctity of Human Life
Stewardship
Media Integrity

At their website, you can learn of AFA's many divisions, which include, American Family Radio, AFR News, Agape Press, and the AFA Journal. These programs and publications can provide links for both ministers and members to find help in resisting sinful behavior jointly within the church and in the world.

In an article that appeared in the April 2005 AFA Journal titled, "Why Caring About Culture Is No Waste of Time," AFA President, Tim Wildmon, wrote:

A recent e-mail to me read: 'My pastor says spending time and energy trying to 'clean up' television is a waste of time. He says we need to spend our time on the Lord's work and doing things that would bring people to salvation in Christ. Since your organization tries to clean up TV, what is your response to this?'

This is a good question. Yes, I've heard it many times over the years, but it's still a good question.

Of course, my first reaction—which comes from the flesh—is, 'Oh yeah, well you can tell your pastor that America is going to hell in a hand basket because of attitudes like that.'

But I don't react like that anymore. Instead, I try to respond in the Spirit. So, let us more closely examine the pastor's criticism.

(Breathe deep before continuing.)

First of all, to say that AFA is just trying to clean up television is really an oversimplification of what we do here. Certainly, the influence of entertainment, especially on America's youth, is of great concern to us, but that is only *one* aspect of our work.

If you have been a supporter of AFA, you know this to be true. Just read through this *Journal* (April 2005) and you will see that we address many moral issues that affect families:

- AFA's Center for Law & Policy defends the constitutional rights of Christians as evidenced in the front page story ("Philly 4 are Free").

- AFA operates a 183-station radio network (American Family Radio), which not only presents the gospel in both music and message, but also informs Christians about what is going on in our country and what they can do to make a difference in the culture war. As a part of AFR, we have a news department to report the news from a Christian perspective, instead of the anti-Christian perspective of the liberal secular media.

- AFA has an online news service called AgapePress that is a Christian version of the Associated Press.

- AFA Journal mails to approximately 145,000 homes nationwide each month.

- AFA maintains several Internet websites including *onemillionmoms.com* and *onemilliondads.com*. These online activist sites have been effective in getting many television advertisers to abandon trashy shows, and encouraging them to use their advertising money more responsibly.

- AFA was one of the pioneers in Internet filtering of pornography (*www.afafilter.com*).

But with respect to fighting back against the tide of immorality in the media, are we, in fact, 'wasting our time' as the pastor says? Here is my response: It is often a thankless job, but someone has to do it.

One can argue (and I suppose the pastor would) that there are more important things addressed by the Christian community, and I would certainly understand that. However, given the enormous power of Hollywood to affect popular culture, it seems to me that there have to be organized efforts that serve as a counterbalance. To raise a standard. To be salt and light, if you will.

We believe the cultural and personal impact of music, movies, and television is real. For example, the promiscuity on TV shows leads to more promiscuity in real life.

Want proof? If television does not have a powerful impact, then why do companies spend millions of dollars on advertisements? They understand the power of the message and the medium, and so should we.

So, while Christians must avoid unwholesome entertainment in their personal lives, we also have a deep concern for our culture. That's why we care about the content of television shows, movies, music, etc. It affects us all.

Again, God may call other Christians to more important work. I would not argue that. But I contend that striving to preserve a healthy moral environment for our children and our grandchildren is no waste of time.

To learn more about the many ways that American Family Association can help your congregation and the families of your church maintain a healthy moral environment, you can go to *www.afa.net*.

5

Dead Sardis Church
THE MESSAGE TO SARDIS

"To the angel of the church in Sardis write:

"These are the words of him who holds the seven spirits of God and the seven stars. I know your deeds; you have a reputation of being alive, but you are dead. Wake up! Strengthen what remains and is about to die, for I have not found your deeds complete in the sight of my God. Remember, therefore, what you have received and heard; obey it, and repent. But if you do not wake up, I will come like a thief, and you will not know at what time I will come to you.

"Yet you have a few people in Sardis who have not soiled their clothes. They will walk with me, dressed in white, for they are worthy. He who overcomes will, like them, be dressed in white. I will never blot out his name from the book of life, but will acknowledge his name before my Father and his angels. He who has an ear, let him hear what the Spirit says to the churches" (Rev. 3:1–6).

The Background of Sardis

Sardis was located about fifty miles east of Smyrna. The

earliest city stood on a 1,000-foot hill five miles south of the Hermus River, the basin of which was the broadest and most fertile of the river valleys of Asia Minor. Sardis commanded the great trade and military road from the Aegean islands to the interior of the Roman provinces of Asia and Galatia. Sardis was thus a thriving city, featuring merchants from all over the world, soldiers of the empire, and others who visited it on a regular basis. Sardis, however, was a sinful city, with a reputation for immorality and open aberrant sexual relationships.

Sardis first achieved greatness as the capital of Lydia. Lydians were employed as mercenaries by the Egyptians (see Jer. 46:8–9 and Ezek. 30:4–5). Lydia was a prosperous kingdom with its capital at Sardis. However, Cyrus of Persia conquered their last king, Croesus, in 546 B.C. Sardis fell after the Persian period to the Athenians, the Seleucids, and the Attalids until bequeathed to the Romans in 133 B.C. Under the Roman Empire, it was the metropolitan capital and center of judicial administration of the Roman province of Lydia.

Destroyed by a powerful earthquake in A.D. 17, Sardis was rebuilt by Tiberius (Caesar during the youth, adulthood, and crucifixion of Christ) and was a thriving, sinful city when John addressed the church there (Rev. 3:1–6).

Part I: Jesus' Negative Evaluation of the Church at Sardis

Christ's letter to Sardis through the Apostle John was one of the most critical communications of the seven letters He wrote. It was almost all negative, and only mentioned a few in the church who avoided being among the spiritually dead! He targeted most of the members and spiritual leaders of this church for being spiritually dead. These were professing Christians who followed the traditions of the church, who "looked" like Christians who worshipped God, but whose names were written in the church rolls but not in heaven's roll book: *"I know your deeds; you have a reputation of being alive, but you are dead"* (Rev. 3:1).

These walking dead people wore *"soiled"* clothing (Rev. 3:4), so we know they were spiritually dead, because the white clothing they wore (their outward appearance of piety) was stained with unconfessed sin. Their spiritual death was due to unforgiven sin, so God was cut off from each soiled clothing wearer and, while they were physically alive, they were spiritually dead.

According to the Greek historian Herodotus, the people of Sardis acquired a reputation for lax moral standards and public immorality over the course of many years. Perhaps, gradually, imperceptibly, this secret sin permeated professing Christians in Sardis, until the Sardis Church membership and spiritual leaders managed to wear many sin-soiled garments (with the stains hidden). "Sin-soiled" garments suggest that beneath the pious professing Christian exterior lurked a secret uncleanness. Not only was there the sin of playing church but also moral sin was covered up.

In Christ's critique of the Sardis Church, He noted two big negatives: (1) good works to try to earn points with God and (2) hypocritical profession of Christianity. However, we notice that this church had no problem with false teachers like the churches in Pergamum and Thyatira. No immoral doctrine of Nicolaitans or Balaam infested the Sardis Church. There was no major false prophet like Jezebel here. Instead, Sardis was outwardly a thriving church. People flocked there each Sunday. But it was a church of hypocrites—actors and actresses—who looked outwardly great but were spiritually dead inside.

Part II: Jesus' Corrective Command to the Church at Sardis

Then, Christ focused on those He labeled as "dead Christians":

"Wake up! Strengthen what remains and is about to die, for I have not found your deeds complete in the sight of my God. Remember, therefore, what you have received and heard; obey it, and repent. But if you do not wake up, I will come like a thief, and you will not know at what time I will come to you" (Rev. 3:3).

Notice the five rapid corrective commands in verses two and three that Christ delivers to the church at Sardis:

1. *"WAKE UP!"* These professing believers were spiritually asleep. They thought they were all right with God. In reality, they slumbered from Sunday to Sunday. Their Christianity wasn't alive and thriving; it was dead! They needed to wake up to their true spiritual condition.

2. *"STRENGTHEN what remains!"* "Strengthen" is the same Greek root word translated as "training" in Ephesians 6:4 ("Fathers, do not exasperate your children; instead, bring them up in the *training* and instruction of the Lord"). It refers to spiritual training of children—here in Sardis, spiritual *children*. They need the milk (doctrinal basics) of the Word of God that they may grow spiritually (see 1 Pet. 2:2). After they awaken from their play church, they need retraining in the basics of their faith so they can accept

Christ as their Savior, and then have a strong biblical foundation upon which to build spiritually. Though Christ mentions the need for strengthening here, it won't be possible until the last command He gives is obeyed.

3. ***"REMEMBER . . . what you have received and heard!"*** After they awaken spiritually and are retrained in the basics of the Bible, then they need to check their memory banks to recall what they received and heard about the message of salvation and discipleship from a Christian evangelist long ago. Because of hidden sin, their old natures control their lives and will keep them in the dark about Bible basics. Remembering their former righteous teaching won't be possible until the last command He gives is obeyed.

4. ***"OBEY it!"*** They are not simply to remember the gospel and discipleship message, but to *obey* this message. They are to act upon what they remember. However, obedience won't be possible until the last command He gives is obeyed.

5. ***"REPENT!"*** When they are convicted of sin, they need to acknowledge it and repent of it with all their hearts. It is a sin to play church and pretend to be Christians. It is a sin to be spiritually dead while proclaiming spiritual life. Only when sinners obey this last command can the previous commands be obeyed. Only when sinners repent of their sin do they find spiritual strength, remember their former righteous path, and find power to obey the Lord. It would appear that most of the members of this church

were professing Christians only, and did not possess
Him as their personal Savior.

Christ said that those He labeled as dead Christians still had a
slight flicker of flame within (the genuine was almost extinguished
from their inner lives, where hypocrisy was aflame). Those flickers
could be fanned by repenting of their sin of rejection of Christ,
accepting Christ as their Savior, then waking up, strengthening,
remembering, and obeying the Lord! They needed to return to
the true doctrine they were taught in the past after repenting of
their sin of turning away from this. Though, the Sardis Church was
dead spiritually (went through worship motions while denying the
power behind them and acting the part of a Christian that was only
an act), there was hope for them—but only if they acknowledged
and turned from their sin of unbelief.

Sardis was the site of the great temple of Artemis, the Greek
goddess of hunting and the moon, and of childbirth (whose Roman
equivalent was Diana). Like Ephesus (see Acts 19:24–29), the
worship of Artemis in Sardis was likely a lucrative trade for those
who made and sold statues to the faithful—and thus hazardous to
Christians who threatened it. However, apparently, no one in the
Sardis Church did anything to threaten this worship. This church
was so dead that they avoided persecution like the plague.

Part III: How Jesus Encouraged Overcomers of the Church at Sardis

*"Yet you have a few people in Sardis who have not soiled
their clothes. They will walk with me, dressed in white,
for they are worthy. He who overcomes will, like them, be
dressed in white. I will never blot out his name from the book
of life, but will acknowledge his name before my Father and
his angels"* (Rev. 3:4–5).

Jesus said one positive thing about a few in the church at Sardis: its righteous remnant. They were Christians who had not soiled themselves with sin stains as the majority in the church had. However, any professing believers, who were soiled by sin, were invited by Him to overcome (repent and be cleansed [forgiven] of their sin, then accept Christ as their personal Savior) and then enjoy the same blessings as the righteous remnant.

Christ made a great promise to the righteous remnant and any who overcame their acting the part of a Christian and secret sins: *"They will walk with me, dressed in white, for they are worthy"* (Rev. 3:4). *"I will never blot out his name from the book of life, but will acknowledge his name before my Father and his angels"* (verse 5).

To walk with Christ, dressed in white, is to be sinlessly pure—an eternal resident of heaven who has free access to Christ. Those who are saved by the blood of the Crucified One during their earthly existence have their names written in permanent ink in God's Book of Life and it will never be erased! Christ will acknowledge all those who placed their faith and trust in Him before God the Father and all God's angelic host in heaven and earth. Heaven's human inhabitants will be like the angels ("At the resurrection people will neither marry nor be given in marriage; they will be like the angels in heaven" [Matt. 22:30]). The glorified bodies of saints will be like the bodies occupied by the angels of God in the absence of a drive to procreate, which is the God-given purpose of marriage (see Eph. 5:31). Believers have an agenda on Earth to reproduce themselves physically and spiritually, but in heaven, only the agenda of Christ matters—the one they can now walk and talk with face to face.

Go back to the beginning of this chapter and reread Revelation 3:1–6. You will read about one huge negative feature of the Sardis Church and one positive feature about a few members only. Now take a brief period to answer the following four questions as they relate to the Sardis Church. Finally, answer the fifth question about your local church. Check Y for yes, N for no, CD for cannot determine, and DK for do not know. (Check the answers under this exercise only after you have answered each question as best you can.)

1-Does the *worship* of members of the Sardis Church please Christ?
__Y __N __ CD __DK
2-Does the *work* of members of the Sardis Church please Christ?
__Y __N __ CD __DK
3-Does the *witness* of members of the Sardis Church please Christ?
__Y __N __ CD __DK
4-What about the Sardis Church displeases Christ?

_____

5-Which negatives about the Sardis Church are present in your local church?

_____

(Answers: 1-CD [nothing is said about worship] or N [implied], 2-N [empty deeds for most] and Y [for a few godly members], 3-CD [nothing is said about witnessing] or N [implied], 4-They profess spiritual life and authenticity, but are spiritually dead and hidden sinners, 5-Answers will vary.)

DEAD SARDIS CHURCH

Now, let's see how the Sardis Church might answer the same questions for which you just filled out answers.

Dear members and leaders of the Church in Sardis, what are your answers to the following three questions?

Does the *worship* of members of your church please Christ?

Does the *work* of members of your church please Christ?

Does the *witness* of members of your church please Christ?

The spiritual leaders of this church, suffering a bad case of spiritual blindness, would probably answer all the questions a resounding, "Yes!"

The members of this church who are in the vast majority of those who attend it, suffering the same affliction as their leaders, would probably answer all the questions another resounding, "Yes!"

However, the few members of this church who are alive spiritually would know that the answers for most of the members and spiritual leaders should be, "No!" They would also know that only the tiny righteous remnant within the church could answer the questions in the affirmative.

The Sardis Church had a reputation of being a church that was spiritually alive, but this description was meaningless. Their church actually was only as spiritually animated as a corpse!

What are the primary concerns of churches like the Sardis Church each Lord's Day? Aren't they something like this:

113

- Are all the lights on and is the place as clean as it can be? (These are important concerns, but they are all-consuming concerns of those interested in externals.)

- Do we have enough people to flip all the switches this week?

- Will this Sunday's sermon make us and any visitors feel good?

- How much entertainment can we enjoy in the service today?

- Can we go through the motions of a church that is alive?

Is a church like this dead or alive?

Jesus said, *"You have a reputation of being alive, but you are dead"* (Rev. 3:1). You have the reputation, but you don't have the life. You're phony!

There Is Hope for Churches Like the Sardis Church

Yet, there is hope for this church, because Jesus also said, *"You have a few people in Sardis who have not soiled their clothes"* (Rev. 3:4). "A few" in this church are not guilty of dead orthodoxy. However, most of the members of this church are dead to any usefulness to Christ, and the church itself is dead, though it professes otherwise.

Christ said that a tiny spark still existed in the hearts of the people, but if it wasn't soon fanned into flame (so repentance and salvation occurred), it would be extinguished forever! He was coming in judgment "like a thief" with no advance warning of His appearance (Rev. 3:3). This means that the "dead" members and leaders of the Sardis Church faced sudden physical death and being ushered into a Christless eternity if they did not quickly act on Christ's warning to them.

Even though the church at Sardis was dead, Jesus could bring it back from the grave. After all, Jesus was the "Resurrection and the Life" (John 11:25). Only days before His own resurrection, Jesus told His disciples: "Our friend Lazarus has fallen asleep; but I am going there to wake him up" (John 11:11). Yet, Jesus delayed reaching Bethany until four days after Lazarus' burial. Jesus purposely waited until He could be certain that Lazarus was dead and buried. He planned to "wake him up" from death to life.

Lazarus' sister, Martha, came out of the house of mourning to greet Him and said, "Lord, if you had been here, my brother would not have died. But I know that even now God will give you whatever you ask" (John 11:21–22).

Martha had faith in Jesus' resurrection power. She knew that He could perform miracles of healing and had raised the dead (the daughter of Jairus, a synagogue president [Luke 8:49–55], and the son of a widow from Nain [Luke 7:11–15]). The faithful few people left at Sardis had the same kind of faith.

Jesus promised Martha, "Your brother will rise again" (John 11:23). Just as Jesus raised Martha's brother from the dead, so He can raise a dead church like Sardis to new life.

He might say something like this to the righteous remnant of that church: "Your brothers and sisters, who are the members of your church at Sardis, go through a bunch of religious motions empty of real significance. They have turned from the truth of God's Word to ceremonies and rituals just as many Jews who attended synagogues in the first century did. Some also have some pet immoral sins they do their best to hide from everyone.

"Do you want Me to bring them back to life? If they want the same thing and repent of their sin of playing church and secret

IS YOUR CHURCH HEAVENLY?

uncleanness, your brothers and sisters will return to being alive, not dead, to Me. Once they repent and accept Me as their personal Savior, no longer will they profess something that is not true. However, if they delay repenting or refuse to, they face premature physical death because they are guilty of false advertising about life in the family of God."

God wants to have another remnant that is faithful to Him. He wants to restore any church today that is like the one at Sardis in the first century. However, His offer is not going to be tendered indefinitely. He will come in judgment to remove professing Christians who serve satan's interests instead of God's.

Does this sound at all like your church?

- Do you sit in your church services today and wonder when the service will be over so you can get something done at home?

- Do you go to church in order to be entertained by the pastor and worship team?

- Do you think fondly only of the past glory days of your church?

- Do you wonder what if *this* or *that* had happened to keep your church alive?

- Do people at your church keep the grass mowed and the building painted to try to impress God?

- Can your church win a contest for the best looking church in town?

- Are the main people whom you want to notice the physical improvements in your church those who drive by your church each day?

In 546 B.C., Cyrus of Persia stomped his military boots on the city of Sardis and kept them there until 214 B.C., when the Greek general Antiochus wrested the city from him. Then a massive earthquake destroyed the city in A.D. 17 during Roman rule. Sardis was no stranger to upheavals.

We all know how upheavals affect churches. One minute a church consists of a godly neighborhood of believers, and then an upheaval occurs within the doctrinal beliefs of the church. Before the members realize it, their church dies spiritually. Dilution occurs to the doctrine of salvation, and societal issues are the focus of preaching. Traditions become tiresome ruts that members run in Sunday after Sunday. After such upheavals, only a few faithful members survive.

Mary stayed in the house of mourning when Jesus came to see her and her sister after Lazarus' death. Either too depressed or lacking the faith in Jesus to believe that He could raise her brother from the dead, she just stayed inside. It was almost like she and Martha reversed roles from Jesus' previous visit to their home.

That earlier visit saw Mary sitting at Jesus' feet, captivated by His teachings, while Martha stayed inside cleaning the house and preparing for the meal for her guest. Jesus then chided the overworked sister by saying, "Martha, Martha, you are worried and upset about many things, but only one thing is needed. Mary has chosen what is better, and it will not be taken away from her" (Luke 10:41–42).

When our church is dying, don't we feel like Martha did when her sister sat at Jesus' feet? We want to keep busy playing church. We want to keep the church clean to impress visitors (and, of course, God). We want to keep the bills paid and the electric (not spiritual) power on. We want to have a minister—even if it is only part time—who will appeal to us and our visitors with a presentation worthy of Hollywood.

The members of the church at Sardis must have felt something like this. Some of the older members could actually tell how, as babies or young children, they barely survived the great earthquake of A.D. 17, which devastated Sardis. After a major earthquake, there are many aftershocks. Everyone in the church had experienced either the earthquake or big aftershocks or had heard of them. Since excavations reveal a large Jewish colony in Sardis, and the Jews generally had no use for Christians, the godly remnant in the church likely faced the upheaval of persecution from them. Even nominal Christians would be distasteful to orthodox Jews.

Sounds like today—so many changes we cannot control.

After Jesus told Martha that Lazarus would come alive again, she replied, "I know he will rise again in the resurrection at the last day." She expected to be told that Jesus would raise her brother from the dead right then, not that he would come alive in the distant future.

"Jesus said to her, 'I am the resurrection and the life. He who believes in me will live, even though he dies; and whoever lives and believes in me will never die. Do you believe this?'" (John 11:24–26).

Dead Orthodoxy or Alive Spiritually?

Why do people so often answer, "No," to Jesus' question: "Do you believe this?"

I taught in the early 90s a workshop for a number of Presbyterian churches. The workshop was on the AIM Program I developed for growing small groups in the church (see chapter seven). The host church was a Presbyterian church located on a busy interstate exit. Some of the host church's staff and members told me when I arrived to set up the workshop of their plight to survive a dwindling membership. They talked about traffic patterns, demographics, and real estate values. They even talked about the desperate financial needs of the church.

However, never once did I hear the host church's Christians talk about Christ, God's will, or the leading of the Holy Spirit. They were concerned about increasing in numbers, but said nothing about spiritual growth.

Why do we have so little faith?

Five years later, they bulldozed the church where I taught my workshop and erected a Wal-Mart in its place. The church dwindled until it died.

"'Yes, Lord,' she [Martha] told him, 'I believe that you are the Christ, the Son of God, who was to come into the world'" (John 11:27). She knew Jesus' identity, but notice that she did not personalize her faith. It was not: "I believe that You are *my* Messiah." She, like many in the Sardis Church, believed in Christ—but He was not her personal Savior.

"And after she had said this, she went back and called her sister Mary aside. 'The Teacher is here,' she said, 'and is asking for you.' When Mary heard this, she got up quickly and went to him" (John 11:28–29). "When Mary reached the place where Jesus was and saw him, she fell at his feet and said, 'Lord, if you had been here, my brother would not have died'" (verse 32).

Some of the Jews who had come to mourn with Mary likely expressed her own view: "But some of them said, 'Could not he who opened the eyes of the blind man have kept this man from dying?'" (Luke 11:37). Mary believed that the presence of Christ was all that was needed to bring supernatural answers to prayers. However, Jesus did not heal *every* sick person in Israel when He healed those who came to Him. Mary, like her sister, knew Jesus was *the* Messiah, but He was not yet *her* personal Savior.

After Christ raised Lazarus from the dead, "Therefore many of the Jews who had come to visit Mary, and had seen what Jesus did, put their faith in him" (John 11:45). After the miracle of this resurrection, Mary and Martha and many of their friends moved from seeing Jesus as *the* Messiah to *their* Messiah. If the dead members of the Sardis Church would do the same, Christ would raise them from the dead.

A Dying Church Raised to New Life

A neighborhood in Jacksonville, Florida had changed from all white to multiracial, but they hung on to an aging, all-white Methodist congregation. They looked to their bishop for a new pastor.

The bishop responded by sending them a new pastor who had experience in music ministry. Their new spiritual leader had traveled extensively and knew many types of people who called themselves Christians. This new pastor was my cousin.

He started to serve as the church's lead minister, opening the church doors to people from all lifestyles. He designed worship services to be all-inclusive. He reached out to the young, the old, blacks, whites, Hispanics, Asians, and everyone he encountered who needed Jesus Christ in his or her life. After fifteen years, he still leads weekly worship at a church that almost died but now thrives.

Christ told the church at Sardis that they must be *"complete in the sight of my God"* (Rev. 3:2). They were not to play church and hide secret sins anymore; they needed to be like the godly remnant in the church.

Christ calls the church at Sardis to *"Wake up," "strengthen what remains," "remember what you have received," "obey [the Bible],"* and *"repent"* (Rev. 3:2–3). If others do what a few in the Sardis church have done, they will *"walk with me, dressed in white, for they are worthy. He who overcomes will, like them, be dressed in white. I will never blot out his name from the book of life, but will acknowledge his name before my Father and his angels"* (verses 4–5).

As I walked through the ruins at Capernaum during my week in Israel, I realized that the very birthplace of Jesus' ministry in Galilee showed little, if any, living evidence of His mission today. Sure, the Christian tourist attractions and the old churches grace the road around the Sea of Galilee but, when you go to Tiberius, you find no living evidence of Christianity.

Did we let our faith die at its foundation?

Does the death of Christianity spread from Jerusalem to Rome? If so, how can we stop its silent, slow demise?

We stop this death the same way it is spreading—one church at a time.

So, if you have identified your church with the church at Sardis, then ask Jesus to come and wake up your church.

Ask Jesus to call your church from the grave.

Thank Jesus for dressing those who overcome in some of those heavenly white clothes.

Ask Jesus to send you out to spread the Gospel.

Ask Jesus to show you how to become God's church—a heavenly church.

"He who has an ear, let him hear what the Spirit says to the churches" (Rev. 3:6).

Your church may need to ask Jesus to raise its people from spiritual death.

Suggestions for the Local Church

What is needed to keep the members and pastors of churches from playing church and practicing secret sins? If a church is dead like the one at Sardis, then it needs to be resurrected by a program like the *40 Days of Purpose* by Rick Warren. If a church wants to prevent spiritual deadness, then it needs to be revitalized by a program like the *40 Days of Purpose.*

From Rick Warren's website, *PurposeDriven.com,* he writes on the campaign web page that:

We believe a healthy, balanced church helps develop changed lives – people who are driven by the five biblical purposes that God designed for every human life.

To introduce the biblical principles behind *The Purpose Driven Life,* we created an intensive church-wide spiritual growth campaign called *40 Days of Purpose.* It's been used by tens of thousands of churches around the world. Through *40 Days of Purpose,* millions of people are now living lives of purpose, transformed by the power of God's grace. They've been baptized as believers in Christ, welcomed into church fellowship, connected to a small group or Sunday school class for discipleship, taught how to approach God in sincere and authentic worship, equipped for ministry and service to others, and commissioned to fulfill their unique, God-appointed mission to the world.

40 Days of Purpose will help your congregation focus on the Kingdom of God, showing each member how to join God in his work throughout the world. Nothing brings more glory to God than having his people fulfill his purpose on earth. The goal, then, is not to simply take your congregation through *40 Days of Purpose;* we believe it will compel your members toward Kingdom work that is greater than any individual, single congregation, or successful denomination. As the Body of Christ, we must all work together "to serve God's purpose in our generation" (Acts 13:36).

As God's purposes are lived out by every believer, practiced in every small group, and fulfilled by every church, imagine the difference it will make in the world! Friend, these are the most exciting days to be alive! We believe this is the beginning of a holy movement, involving churches of all shapes and sizes working together toward the same purpose. I know your heart is lead to your congregation toward greater Kingdom work, and I believe that *40 Days of Purpose* will help you in your efforts. It was a powerful discipleship tool at Saddleback; I've seen it work in thousands of other churches across the globe; and I believe it will be effective in your church. Will you allow us to partner with you as you prepare for the Kingdom work ahead?

As millions of people already know, this is certainly the kind of program that will awaken and revitalize a dead or dying church like Sardis. *The Purpose-Driven Life* opens with the statement that "this is more than a book; it is a guide to a *40-day spiritual journey* that will enable you to discover the answer to life's most important question: What on earth am I here for? By the end of this journey you will know God's purpose for your life and will understand the big picture—how all the pieces of your life fit together. Having this perspective will reduce your stress, simplify your decisions, increase your satisfaction, and, most important, prepare you for eternity."[1]

When church pastors, church leaders, and church members complete a program like the *40 Days of Purpose* they will not be dead, but alive to Christ and His Church. They will come to understand the God's Kingdom purpose in their lives and that as Rick Warren wrote in the close of *The Purpose Driven Life* "God wants to use you."

Warren wrote that "About thirty years ago, I noticed a little phrase in Acts 13:36 that forever altered the direction of my life. It was only seven words but, like the stamp of a searing hot branding iron, my life was permanently marked by these words: "David served God's purpose in his generation" (Acts 13:36a). Now I understood why God called David "a man after my own heart" (Acts 13:22). David dedicated his life to fulfilling God's purpose on earth.

"There is no greater epitaph than that statement! Imagine it chiseled on *your* tombstone: That *you* served God's purpose in your generation. My prayer is that people will be able to say that about me when I die. It is why I wrote this book to you. This phrase is the ultimate definition of a life well lived. You do the eternal and timeless (God's purpose) in a contemporary and timely way (in your generation). That is what the *purpose-driven life* is all about."[2]

Imagine what your church and every church would be like if the pews were filled with people living out the purpose driven life seen in Rick Warren. We would have no dead churches like Sardis. We would only have churches that were alive to Jesus Christ. To learn more about all the many *Purpose Driven* books and programs you can go to *www.purposedriven.com.*

6
Faithful Philadelphia Church
THE MESSAGE TO PHILADELPHIA

"To the angel of the church in Philadelphia write:

"These are the words of him who is holy and true, who holds the key of David. What he opens no one can shut, and what he shuts no one can open. I know your deeds. See, I have placed before you an open door that no one can shut. I know that you have little strength, yet you have kept my word and have not denied my name. I will make those who are of the synagogue of Satan, who claim to be Jews though they are not, but are liars—I will make them come and fall down at your feet and acknowledge that I have loved you. Since you have kept my command to endure patiently, I will also keep you from the hour of trial that is going to come upon the whole world to test those who live on the earth.

"I am coming soon. Hold on to what you have, so that no one will take your crown. Him who overcomes I will make a pillar in the temple of my God. Never again will he leave it. I will write on him the name of my God and the name of the city of my God, the new Jerusalem, which is coming down out of heaven from my God; and I will also write on him my new name. He who has an ear, let him hear what the Spirit

says to the churches" (Rev. 3:7–13).

The Background of Philadelphia

Philadelphia was a city of Lydia located 26 miles east of Sardis by the Roman road. It stood on a broad hill 800 feet in altitude on the imperial post road that came from Rome via Troas and led eastward through Phrygia. Location on an important trade route and control of a great grape-growing district contributed greatly to Philadelphian prosperity. The importance of Philadelphia dates from about 150 B.C., when Attalus II Philadelphus of Pergamum refounded the original city. The king was so named from his devotion to his brother Eumenes, and the city perpetuated his title (Philadelphia is Greek for "brotherly love").

The earthquake of A.D. 17 that destroyed Sardis also destroyed Philadelphia; Tiberius gave large sums for its rebuilding along with other destroyed cities in the area.

John addressed the church in Philadelphia (Rev 3:7–13), but without the help of an excavation there, it is difficult to recreate a view of the city, as the apostle knew it. Yet, from the letter by Christ to this city, we know that Jews populated a large area of Philadelphia. We can assume that the Roman citizens were similar to other natives in nearby cities: thus, treating Christians who refused to worship Caesar with contempt.

There is an Islamic village today on the ancient site of Philadelphia that is called Allah Shehr ("City of God").

Compare the Letters to Philadelphia and Four Other Churches

Does this letter from Christ sound anything like the letter He wrote to the Ephesus Church? In that letter, which we examined in chapter one, Christ praised a number of things that the members and leaders were doing to please God, but He had one huge issue against them: they had lost their first love for Him.

Does this letter from Christ resemble the letter He wrote to the Pergamum Church? In that letter, which we examined in chapter three, Christ praised a few things that the members and leaders were doing to please God, but He had two big issues against them: they tolerated the false doctrines of immorality and idolatry.

Does this letter from Christ look anything like the letter He wrote to the Thyatira Church? In that letter, which we examined in chapter four, Christ praised a number of things that the members and leaders were doing to please God, but He had the same issues as those in Pergamum against them: they not only tolerated the false doctrines of immorality and idolatry, but employed a false teacher who taught these doctrines of satan in the church.

Does this letter from Christ suggest anything in the letter He wrote to the Sardis Church? In that letter, which we examined in chapter five, Christ said that except for a few righteous members, the vast majority of the church people were spiritually dead: they followed empty traditions and were hypocrite Christians.

Now check out the letter in Revelation 3:7–13 again, and determine how many issues you can find in it that Christ had against those in the other four churches just mentioned?

You searched for something that is *nowhere* to be found in this letter. Christ said *nothing* negative about those in the Philadelphia Church! He did the same in His second letter, which was addressed to the Smyrna Church. The other five letter recipients read one or more negative statements from the Writer. However, His only direct comments about the behavior of the Philadelphia believers were positive. He evaluated them as being faithful believers who stood up for Him as they faced Jewish and pagan enemies of their faith. However, even though Christ said nothing negative about the believers in the Philadelphia Church, He said nothing positive about their enemies. Notice the following six features of this uplifting letter to the Philadelphia Church:

Part I: Jesus' Six Positive Evaluations of the Church at Philadelphia

1. *"These are the words of him who is holy and true, who holds the key of David. What he opens no one can shut, and what he shuts no one can open."* Christ says that He is holy and true (personifies the righteousness of God) and holds the key of David. In Isaiah 22:15–20, we learn that God, after ousting the present steward over King Hezekiah's household, chose Eliakim, the son of the palace administrator, to fill the position. God called Eliakim "a father to those who live in Jerusalem and to the house of Judah," adding: "I will place on his shoulder the **key to the house of David;** what he opens no one can shut, and what he shuts no one can open" (Isaiah 22:21–22). *Eliakim* means, "God has established," and foreshadows Christ, the Head of God's household. The keys of David are the divine authority to open and close the doors to God's household in heaven. When Christ opens this door, no one can close it. In other words, no one is such a rotten sinner that he cannot enter heaven's door. When Christ closes this door, no one can open it: a time is coming when this door will close either at the death of a lost person or the rejection so often of salvation that a person becomes insensitive to the invitation (the "sin that leads to death" of 1 John 5:16).

2. *"I know your deeds."* Christ knew (and commended)

128

the actions of all the Christians in the Philadelphia Church. Commended deeds would have been evidences of the fruit of the Spirit, which are "love, joy, peace, patience, kindness, goodness, faithfulness, gentleness and self-control" (Gal. 5:22–23). These were Christians who were characterized by godly behavior. They did not do good works in order to show off. Instead, they did good deeds for as many other people as they could, seeking to demonstrate their Christianity to them.

3. *"I know that you have little strength, yet you have kept my word and have not denied my name."* Christ knew that the Philadelphia Church had little influence on the city of "Brotherly Love." It has been suggested that the congregation was small and composed mainly of the lower classes of Roman society. This does not mean that the Christians in Philadelphia were spiritually weak, but simply that they had little strength in influencing their society because many Romans would ignore lower classes of society. Nonetheless, these believers faithfully studied, then obeyed God's Word and took stands for Christ rather than recanting when faced with persecution. They were men and women of the Word of God, who demonstrated spiritual strength but had a limited influence on their pagan society, who treated Christians with contempt.

4. *"I will make those who are of the synagogue of Satan, who claim to be Jews though they are not, but are liars—I will make them come and fall down at your feet and acknowledge that I have loved you."* Orthodox Jews were the source of considerable

persecution in Philadelphia. They made life difficult for Christians. They had no room for Christ or for anyone who reminded them of Him. So fanatical was the Jewish opposition to their Messiah, that Christ labeled them a *"synagogue of Satan."* They no doubt labeled themselves a "synagogue of God." However, Christ promised here to make the lying Jews (who mislabeled themselves as "godly Jews") *"come and fall down at your feet and acknowledge that I have loved you."* In other words, He promised that among the synagogue members, some would come to faith in Christ as their Messiah. Some who treated Christians with contempt would realize their error and embrace Gentile members of their new family. As the Christians in Philadelphia move out with the gospel message in the future, Christ promises them some success in their Jewish evangelism.

5. ***"Since you have kept my command to endure patiently, I will also keep you from the hour of trial that is going to come upon the whole world to test those who live on the earth."*** Christ prophesied that the believers in Philadelphia would soon face even worse persecution than at the present time. The *"hour of trial"* that is to come *"upon the whole [Roman] world to test those who live on the earth"* is a time of severe trial for all Christians in the Roman Empire in the later first century–early second century, as Christianity becomes an illegal religion of the Roman Empire and persecution intensifies against Christians. (Notice that this is the *"hour of trial,"* not "tribulation." The Great Tribulation is not in view here.) Christ promises to the faithful believers at Philadelphia that they will be

protected from this future period of dangerous trial for Christians.

6. *"I am coming soon. Hold on to what you have, so that no one will take your crown."* Christ promises the faithful members of the Philadelphia Church that He is coming soon, so they need to hold on to what they have—their faithfulness and willingness to suffer persecution for their faith; their good works, living faith, regular Bible study, and evangelism—so that no other Christian will take their crown of reward. In other words, that they continue to live active Christian lives and don't become complacent and stop witnessing while they await Christ's coming. They need to hold on to what Christ has given them and invest it for eternity, rather than burying their talent and letting another faithful believer take it (see Matt. 25:18, 28).

The first feature Christ stated about the believers in Philadelphia was their good works. Their good works were the fruit of the Spirit. The fruit of the Spirit is a quality of the members of a heavenly church.

A second feature that Christ said about the believers in Philadelphia was their faithfulness in witnessing, no matter how it was received. Due to their low position in Roman Society, the Roman citizens of Philadelphia didn't take them seriously. Yet, they were faithful witnesses, no matter how they were received. Witnessing, no matter how it is received, is a quality of the members of a heavenly church.

A third feature that Christ said about the believers in Philadelphia was their faithfulness to the Lord under oppression. They were faithful to lose their lives rather than their faith. Willingness to suffer persecution for your faith is a quality of the members of a heavenly church.

A **fourth feature** that Christ said about the believers in Philadelphia was their persecution by the Jewish synagogue. They were the special targets of orthodox Jews. Persecution by the enemies of Christ is a characteristic of the members of a heavenly church.

A **fifth feature** that Christ said about the believers in Philadelphia was their active Christian testimony. They were faithful to take a stand for Christ and never deny Him. Willingness to take a stand for Christ and never deny Him is a quality of the members of a heavenly church.

Part II: How Jesus Encouraged Overcomers of the Church at Philadelphia

1. *"Him who overcomes I will make a pillar in the temple of my God. Never again will he leave it. I will write on him the name of my God and the name of the city of my God, the new Jerusalem, which is coming down out of heaven from my God; and I will also write on him my new name."* Those who are victorious in Philadelphia will become pillars of the temple of God, and "they will never leave" this building. The *"temple of my God"* is not the whole temple structure. All sixteen references to the temple in Revelation (3:12; 7:15; 11:1, 19 [twice]; 14:15, 17; 15:5–6, 8 [twice]; 16:1, 17, and 22 [twice]) use the word that designates the inner shrine rather than the larger precincts. It is the place where God's presence dwells: the Holy Place. Thus, the Philadelphia pillars are in the presence of God in heaven for eternity. They have written on their foreheads the name of God and of God's Son (see

Rev. 14:1 and 22:4). Christ's *"new name"* symbolizes all that He is by virtue of His redemptive work for mankind and awaits the Second Advent before it will be revealed. Christ also mentions that the name of the New Jerusalem will be written on the Philadelphian saints. In heaven, believers are identified as eternal citizens who have communion with their Creator and their Savior. Those who will live in the New Jerusalem after the Second Advent are also identified with the name of their future dwelling place.

Reread Revelation 3:7–13 at the beginning of this chapter. Now take a brief period to answer the following four questions about the Philadelphia Church. Finally, answer the fifth question about your local church. Check Y for yes, N for no, CD for cannot determine, and DK for do not know. (Check the answers under this exercise only after you have answered each question as best you can.)

1-Does the *worship* of members of the Philadelphia Church please Christ?

__Y __N __CD __DK

2-Does the *work* of members of the Philadelphia Church please Christ?

__Y __N __CD __DK

3-Does the *witness* of members of the Philadelphia Church please Christ?

__Y __N __CD __DK

4-What about the Philadelphia Church displeases Christ?

_____

5-Which features of the Philadelphia Church are present in your local church?

_____

(Answers: 1-Y, 2-Y, 3-Y, 4-Nothing, 5-Answers will vary.)

Prayer for Heavenly Churches in the World

When I was in Galilee on Monday, January 24, 2005, I made my final morning visit to the return site at Daliyyot. Then, when I returned to my motel to write the first part of chapter six of this book (I wrote about the letters to the churches in a different order than they occur in Revelation), I wrote these words: At Daliyyot this morning, I prayed, "Christ in me, Christ in the world" right after praying, "Come, Lord Jesus, come." After the previous six days of writing, I had come to realize that if Jesus did not return in the flesh on the 25th, I needed to make every effort to carry His message of reformation for the churches into the world.

My special prayer after my regular prayer was a request for God to use my experience in Galilee to bring the words and the light of Jesus Christ into as many churches as I could. For me personally, I have always longed to live Paul's words that for me "to live is Christ" (for Christ to live through my life) (Gal. 2:20). This prayer is that heavenly churches may occur worldwide. The book you hold is God's answer to my prayer.

Demonstrations of Christ's Love

The church at Philadelphia ("brotherly love" in Greek) demonstrated brotherly love to others through the power of Jesus Christ. We can recognize churches like Philadelphia that are filled with Christ's love when we visit them. Christians warmly greet us. Christians smile at us and make us feel welcome. Many people want to be a part of this kind of fellowship.

So we join and grow with these loving congregations. We recognize the fruits of this new friendship when members of our new spiritual family reach out to us, visit us, and rejoice when we rejoice and suffer when we suffer.

Jesus said, "Whatever you did for one of the least of these brothers of mine, you did for me" (Matt. 25:40). As a member of a loving, faithful church like Philadelphia, we experience numerous opportunities for others to do to good things for us and for us to do to good deeds for others. We develop many friends in our church. In time, we realize that the love of friendship grows into the love of family, and we now experience the closeness of many sisters and brothers in Christ. We knew when we entered the family of God that every other true Christian was either our brother or sister but, through friendship and love of our church family, this proposition becomes warmly personalized.

Jesus informed His disciples, "In my Father's house are many rooms; if it were not so, I would have told you. I am going there to prepare a place for you. And if I go and prepare a place for you, I will come back and take you to be with me that you also may be where I am. You know the way to the place where I am going" (John 14:2–4).

I will never forget preaching my first funeral. I had only visited this church member twice, yet I knew that the family hungered for words to bring them comfort and hope. However, I was keenly aware as I officiated that my past experiences and my previous training had not prepared me to deal with this very important time in the lives of this church member's family. I had never attended a Bible college or seminary. I presented a familiar Bible message, but I had no idea how to make the message personal and comforting to the loved ones. I was a little like Thomas—in a quandary about what the future held.

Thomas said to him, "Lord, we don't know where you are going, so how can we know the way?

Jesus answered him, "I am the way and the truth and the life. No one comes to the Father except through me" (John 14:5–6).

The pastors in my church community practiced what I termed

136

"Salvation Verification," whereby they would rush to a dying person's bedside to confirm that person's saving belief in Jesus Christ. Or, if they could not confirm a salvation before death, the pastor would contact former pastors of the person to verify the individual's acceptance of Jesus Christ as his or her Lord and Savior and his or her entry into heaven.

I had some sleepless nights over this theological dilemma. Then, I realized that the Holy Spirit is Christ's Heavenly Agent in the world, not me. In other words, I did not have to verify if a dead person had accepted Christ. Only the Holy Spirit knows a person's spiritual condition for sure. Though I could look for spiritual fruit in a person's life, I could be fooled. The Holy Spirit, on the other hand, can never be fooled. Praise God!

When someone professes faith in Jesus Christ, he or she joins the family of God and becomes a citizen of heaven that very day.

Christ dictates to John: *"I have placed before you an open door that no one can shut"* (Rev. 3:8). In 2 Corinthians 2:12, the Apostle Paul said, "Now when I went to Troas to preach the gospel of Christ . . . the Lord had **opened a door** for me." Paul wrote to the Corinthians, "I will stay on at Ephesus until Pentecost, because **a great door** for effective work **has opened** to me, and there are many who oppose me" (1 Cor. 16:8–9).

The "door" that Christ opened for the Philadelphia Church that no one can close is the door of opportunity to preach the gospel. It is the same door opened for Paul in Troas and Ephesus. No matter the circumstances, these first century Christians find an open door for the gospel message. Christ challenges His followers to invite other people to His great home, because He has opened the door to heaven. Jesus reminds the Philadelphia Church family of their qualifications and their call to evangelism when He says, *"You have kept my word and have not denied my name. I will make those who are of the synagogue of Satan, who claim to be Jews though they are not, but are liars — I will make them come and fall down at your feet and acknowledge that I have loved you"* (Rev. 3:8–9).

Jesus sends the church at Philadelphia and all other loving, faithful congregations into the world to seek members for God's heavenly family.

Jesus says, "I am the [door]" (John 10:7, 9). And, we, His Church, must tell our neighbors that the door to heaven stands open in our church and beckons to everyone to accept Christ as his or her personal Savior.

Jesus says, "I am the [door]." And, we, His Church, must tell our neighbors that eternal life is available at our church and to those who accept Christ as their personal Savior.

Jesus says, "I am the [door]." And, we, His Church, must tell our neighbors that Christ has prepared a room in heaven for each person who accepts Him as his or her personal Savior.

On Sunday morning in Galilee, I went to mass at Tabgha, a town a few miles north of Tiberius, where I stayed. I wanted to go to a Protestant church in Tiberius, but when I asked about it at the motel desk, the clerk had nothing good to say about the Protestant church there and referred me to the Catholic Church in Tabgha. When I arrived at the Church of the Multiplication of the Loaves and Fishes, I discovered a beautiful courtyard outside the sanctuary that had benches, flowers, walkways, and a gift shop. The stone-wall sanctuary had a high ceiling, and I joined thirteen others at the service on wooden benches. The officiating priest invited us to sit around the communion table and told us that the service would be in German, with a little English (in reality, only two statements were this).

We listened as the priest preached from Matthew 4:12–23, where Jesus began His ministry here in Galilee. I did not understand German, but I was familiar with this passage of Scripture and waited for the English words.

After the priest said, in English, "The people living in darkness have seen a great light" (quoting Matt. 4:16), I said, "Amen!" Then he said, continuing verse sixteen in English, "On those living in the land of the shadow of death a light has dawned." I said, "Amen and Amen!"

After the mass, one of the five nuns who attended the service asked me, "Are you an evangelist?" The nun may have thought I was one of the attendees at an evangelism conference that was being held that week in Jerusalem.

"No," I replied, "I'm Presbyterian."

Jesus calls all of the members of the family of God, not just those employed as evangelists, to evangelize (see Acts 1:8).

Jesus calls His church family to invite our neighbors to walk through the open door of heaven by accepting Christ as their personal Savior.

Jesus calls His church family to shine His light into our communities and let His light illuminate the gap between man and God called SIN and the only bridge over the gap, the CROSS of Christ.

"Through him all things were made; without him nothing was made that has been made. In him was life, and that life was the light of men. The light shines in the darkness, but the darkness has not understood it" (John 1:3–5).

Have we shared the Word with the world? Have we shined His light into the spiritual darkness around us?

We, the Church, cannot expect men like Billy and Franklin Graham to shoulder alone the work of evangelism.

We, the Church, must preach the Good News of salvation through Jesus Christ in our pulpits every Sunday.

We, the Church, must shine the light of the gospel into our dark world everyday.

We, the Church, must stand firm in our Christian faith: a faith that provides a rich spiritual life, eternal friends, a loving spiritual family, and an eternal home in heaven.

We, the Church, must cherish these gifts of God's glory and seek to share them with the people in our community.

We, the Church, must live as Christ's family and bring Christ into the world.

Jesus thanks the church at Philadelphia for their good work and tells them that *"I will also keep you from the hour of trial"* and *"I am coming soon"* (Rev. 3:10–11).

"He who has an ear, let him hear what the Spirit says to the churches" (Rev. 3:13).

Christ's Church needs to beckon the lost to the open doors of heaven.

Suggestions for the Local Church
Eternity Is Serious Business

In her book, *HEAVEN Who's Got the Tickets & How Much Do They Cost?* Martha Boshart writes:

Everyday thousands of fates are sealed into an eternity of either heaven or hell. There is often no warning, no fanfare, and particularly no time to prepare. If we're on the road to heaven, having made that decisive journey to the cross, it really doesn't matter. We have already heeded someone's warning about the hell at the end of the road and turned around. The fanfare in heaven already began the moment we fell on our knees at the foot of the cross, conceded our place among lost sinners, and reached up to take possession of God's gift of eternal life. We have our ticket to heaven in hand, written in Jesus' blood and absolutely free.

If we're still on the highway to hell, however, nothing in the world could matter more. Everyone traveling *that* highway eventually ends up in a crash—a crash in which there are no survivors. There are no rescue crews, no ambulances, and no emergency rooms. Everyone is a fatality; there are no exceptions.

And we're all traveling on that highway unless we've been stopped, warned, turned around, or otherwise redirected by someone who is honoring not merely a code, but a commission—the Great Commission:

The Task Is Simple: Go!

That Great Commission was proclaimed over two thousand years ago by Jesus and is recorded in Mark 16:15 (KJV): "Go ye into all the world, and preach the gospel to every creature."

This is not just an assignment; it's a commission. When such an honor is bestowed on someone in the military, everyone involved celebrates. The Great Commission, on the other hand, doesn't lend itself to pomp and celebration. In fact, there is usually no commissioning ceremony, no conspicuous badge to wear, no certificate to display on the wall, no monetary increment in one's paycheck. This commission is a simple, humble, earthly command to share the gospel of Jesus Christ with our world.

The "World" Is Wherever You Are

For some of us, the world where we preach the gospel might be right in our own home or our neighborhood, our workplace, even in our church. For others, it may require taking off to other continents—to exotic hotbeds of sensual charm, or lonely, scary, forbidding jungles. It may mean leaving everyone and everything we know and love and going where everyone is unfamiliar, maybe even unfriendly.

Wherever our world is, knowing someone around us is destined for hell should be compelling in itself. Being commissioned to share the good news that there is another way, another itinerary, and another destination is a truly awesome, invigorating responsibility.

I hope and pray that your church will take on this "invigorating responsibility" of opening the doors of heaven to the people in your community.[1]

For more information on Ms. Boshart's book and to purchase it, you can e-mail Barbour Publishing at *info@barbourbooks.com*.

A Powerful Program of Evangelism

How do we implement an evangelism program that allows our church to experience the "invigorating responsibility" that Boshart talks about?

At the website for Evangelism Explosion, Dr. Adrian Rogers,

the pastor of Bellevue Baptist Church in Memphis, Tennessee (until his death in 2005), is quoted: "For many years Evangelism Explosion has been a dynamic discipleship ministry for Bellevue Baptist Church. More than training members to win people to Jesus, it trains them how to train others to win people to Jesus. This is the essence of the Great Commission, and should be a primary goal of every New Testament church."

Through their website (*www.eeinternational.org*), Evangelism Explosion International offers local churches the following benefits:

An Effective Strategy for Training Your Laypeople to Spread God's Message

Imagine every member of your church actively, boldly, confidently, and daily telling others God's saving story—the Good News. What would happen in the life of your church? Not just growth, but healthy growth—a powerful surge of spiritual maturity in your congregation. This kind of maturity ripens into leadership—the kind of leadership that reaches out to the lost and makes disciples!

Telling People About Jesus Passionately

That's exactly the result when you begin the adventure of using Evangelism Explosion (EE) in your church. There are many concerns in the church today. Most likely topping the list is the lethargy toward lost people and the inability of your people to speak openly about Jesus' message and mission to bring individuals from unbelief to belief.

EE impacts every generation for the work of the Great Commission, from Gen Yer's to Gen-Xer's to seniors. EE's culturally sensitive materials and training are setting hearts afire for the critical work of telling others Jesus' plan of redemption.

"Help Me to Open My Mouth!"

Christians desperately want to reach their world for Christ. And the excitement of teaching them and seeing them mature into leaders is one of the greatest blessings for a pastor. Through a Leadership Training Clinic, EE will prepare you to equip them. In just a few days you'll receive all the resources to gear them up, unleashing your people to help others discover new life in Christ. The EE resources cross denominations, are culturally sensitive, and have proven effective for every generation. When you attend an EE Leadership Training Clinic, you'll explore in depth tough issues like:

- Building a bridge of friendship with the unchurched

- Ascertaining what people believe

- Articulating the Good News briefly and succinctly

- Moving from apathy and timidity to spiritual influence

- Tailoring a Gospel presentation to fit your personality

- Answering the common objections

- Dispelling the #1 killer of boldness—fear

- Moving an unbeliever to belief

No More Spiritual Lethargy

When your members experience EE training, they become

full of spiritual energy. Suddenly they will not fear the unknown, mistrust the untried, or avoid the new. They will draw strength from looking ahead, seeing the lost, having a desire to reach them with the Gospel, discipling them, and turning them into witnesses. That's the power of the Holy Spirit. That's EE.

Unleash the "Missionaries" in Your Pews

Teach them how to tell others Jesus' story and great offer. In just days, an EE Leadership Training Clinic will radically change your life and, ultimately, the life of your church.

When your people's issue the plea, "Pastor, help me communicate Jesus!" are you willing to respond to it? In light of America's precarious situation today, Christians desperately want to experience joy and freedom in telling the Good News. That's what America needs most because our country is fast becoming morally and spiritually bankrupt—the kind of degenerate society that spiritually progressive countries send their missionaries to.

But the fact is that America's "missionaries" are sitting in your pews waiting for someone to disciple them. Then they can dialogue confidently and boldly with their friends, neighbors, relatives, associates, and others who cross their paths about the greatest story ever told—that of the Messiah, Jesus.

In an article titled *Wartime Living* in the EE online publication "Multiply" (#2 / 2004), Dr. D. James Kennedy, Founder and President (who died in 2007), wrote:

Evangelism Explosion through Christ is bringing God's peace to lost people. To employ a biblical metaphor, we are engaged in a war.

James Bradley in "Flags of Our Fathers" graphically describes the sacrifices our whole country made during World War II: "Everyone scrambled to be of help…Americans pitched in to support strict rationing programs…Shoes became scarce… People grew 'victory gardens'...Americans sacrificed."

Fellow Christians, Scripture tells us that there's a war going on in the world today between Christ and satan, truth and falsehood, heaven and hell. Soldiers of the cross need to be supported. Weapons of the Gospel need to be funded. And the stakes of this conflict are higher than any other in history!

Evangelism Explosion is involved in a life-or-death struggle on every continent of the world. On the front lines we are conscripting, equipping and dispatching a new kind of "strategic soldier." He's called an Implementation Field Worker (IFW). He comes alongside pastors who have attended training clinics to help them launch and grow the EE ministry in their churches. As a result of this new field strategy, EE is experiencing unprecedented Christ-honoring victory.

To launch and maintain this new, exciting strategy requires tremendous sacrifice. And our IFWs are committed to such "wartime living."

To bring your church into this "wartime living" and to see Christ make "those who are victorious pillars in the temple of my God," you can go to Evangelism Explosion International's web site at *www.eeinternational.org* and sign up for their Leadership Training Clinic.

7

Lukewarm Laodicea Church
THE MESSAGE TO LAODICEA

"To the angel of the church in Laodicea write:

"These are the words of the Amen, the faithful and true witness, the ruler of God's creation. I know your deeds, that you are neither cold nor hot. I wish you were either one or the other! So, because you are lukewarm — neither hot nor cold — I am about to spit you out of my mouth. You say, 'I am rich; I have acquired wealth and do not need a thing.' But you do not realize that you are wretched, pitiful, poor, blind and naked. I counsel you to buy from me gold refined in the fire, so you can become rich; and white clothes to wear, so you can cover your shameful nakedness; and salve to put on your eyes, so you can see.

"Those whom I love I rebuke and discipline. So be earnest, and repent. Here I am! I stand at the door and knock. If anyone hears my voice and opens the door, I will come in and eat with him, and he with me.

"To him who overcomes, I will give the right to sit with me on my throne, just as I overcame and sat down with my Father on his throne. He who has an ear, let him hear what the Spirit says to the churches" (Rev. 3:14–22).

The Background of Laodicea

There were four cities called Laodicea: (1) In Phrygia, near Hierapolis; (2) In the east of Phrygia; (3) On the coast of Syria, the port of Aleppo; and (4) East of Lebanon. The first is the only one mentioned in Scripture, as one of the seven churches of Revelation. It was an ancient city on the Lycus River in a valley that was forty miles east of Ephesus; it had two names before being called Laodicea. Its site was on seven hills, which were drained by two brooks. The Laodicean ruins that have been excavated by archaeologists are of a stadium in very complete preservation, theaters (three in all; one of which was 400 feet in diameter), bridges, aqueducts, and a gymnasium, all which testify to its ancient wealth and importance. Its original name was Diospolis (the city of Jupiter), which was changed to Rhoas, under which title it became the largest city of Phyrgia. Antiochus II of the Seleucid Kingdom (261-246 BC) gave it the name of his wife, Laodike. He settled it with Syrians and Jews brought from Babylonia.

The city's great wealth came from its commerce and its production of fine quality world-famous black wool. "Phrygian powder" was another source of income; it was a medicine for the eyes, which seems to have come through Laodicea into general use among the Greeks (and was indirectly referred to by Christ in Rev. 3:18). Laodicea was so prosperous that it refused an imperial subsidy when a disastrous earthquake leveled it in A.D. 60. Its citizens rebuilt their city from their own resources. The Lord scored the members of the church at Laodicea for their trust in riches (verse 17).

Laodicea obtained its water from hot springs some distance away through pipes made of cubical blocks of stone three feet across, bound and cemented together. By the time the water reached the city, it was not hot enough for health baths, nor cool enough for drinking, but suitable only for an emetic if drunk (to cause vomiting). This explains the reference in Revelation 3:16 to "neither hot nor cold." Water piped in to Laodicea was lukewarm by the time it reached the city. Thus, people had to heat it for cooking or cool it for drinking.

A church already existed in Laodicea by the time Paul wrote his epistle to the Colossians (A.D. 61–63), although he had not personally visited the city (Col. 2:1). Epaphras' great concern for the Christians there suggests that he may have founded the church (Col. 4:13). Paul requested the Colossian believers to greet the brethren in Laodicea and to exchange letters from him with them (Col. 4:15–16). Paul's epistle to Laodicea was probably lost, as were some others of his letters (cf. 1 Cor. 5:9), although certain devout scholars have argued that the canonical book of Ephesians was originally sent to the Laodiceans before going to Ephesus (this is an argument from silence). The last of John's letters to the seven churches of Asia (Rev. 2–3) was sent to Laodicea. By the time he wrote, the congregation had become largely apostate (Rev 3:14–22). Christians in the church in Laodicea recognized that Christ was describing their spiritual condition by relating it to their well-known inefficient water system.

Part I: Jesus' Negative Evaluation of the Church at Laodicea

1. *"I know your deeds, that you are neither cold nor hot. I wish you were either one or the other!"* Christ says, *"I know your deeds."* He could have added, "They prove that you are apostate believers (your lifestyles renounce your profession of Christianity)." The lukewarm Christian does not become greatly disturbed at hearing heretical teaching and is not

vigorous in the defense of the truth of the Word of
God. This spirit of indifference is the most tragic thing
that can happen to a church. As Christ evaluates the
church in Laodicea, He is dismayed to find it rife with
spiritual indifference—an attitude of apostates. These
professing Christians were not following Christ, who
was never indifferent, but satan, who loves it when
believers are false examples of life in the family of
God.

2. *"You say, 'I am rich; I have acquired wealth and do
not need a thing.' But you do not realize that you are
wretched, pitiful, poor, blind and naked."* The professing
Christians in Laodicea were wealthy and self-
sufficient. Just as they sought no outside assistance
after a disastrous earthquake struck them, so they
considered their physical riches adequate to provide
all their needs in their church. Members were always
well-dressed and their church building well-appointed
but, as Christ looked within each member, He saw
that each one was spiritually wretched (unhappy and
joyless), pitiful (distressed and sad), poor (spiritually
bankrupt), blind (spiritually), and naked (unrighteous
before God). He saw within each member apostasy
and spiritual blindness that prevented the person
from seeing it.

3. *"Because you are lukewarm--neither hot nor cold--
I am about to spit you out of my mouth."* Christ has
no use for spiritual fence-straddlers, for they are a
false advertisement of the family of God as well as
apostates. Since they will not take a stand among the
pagans and orthodox Jews in Laodicea for Christ,

nor will they care if heretical teaching occurs, they are apostate Christians guilty of unconfessed sins they can't recognize because of spiritual blindness. Therefore, as servants not of Christ but of His enemy, satan, He is ready to spit them out of His mouth like they would if they drank the lukewarm water coming from their water pipes. When Christ expectorates distasteful religious people this way, it means their physical lives are ended prematurely (see 1 Cor. 11:29-30). Thus, Christ is threatening to end the lives of spiritual fence-straddlers who serve satan's interests, not His. Are any of these apostates headed for hell? It would seem that some are merely backsliders, but the majority is unsaved. A premature physical end will mean a Christless eternity for all those who are spiritually lost.

Part II: Jesus' Corrective Command to the Church at Laodicea

1. *"I counsel you to buy from me gold refined in the fire, so you can become rich; and white clothes to wear, so you can cover your shameful nakedness; and salve to put on your eyes, so you can see."* Christ refers to three items in which Laodicea took great pride: financial wealth, an extensive textile industry, and a famous eye salve, applying each item in a spiritual sense. The fence-straddling Laodiceans needed spiritual riches that they could only buy from Christ. They needed to make this purchase by surrendering the control of their finances to Him. They also needed to purchase the white clothing of the pure and righteous

by surrendering the control of all their body parts and possessions to Him. A third need was for their spiritual blindness, for they didn't see anything wrong with their spiritual lukewarmness. They needed to purchase spiritual eye salve from Christ for the cost of surrendering their spiritual blindness to Him. Until they paid for the eye salve, they would be blind to their need for spiritual riches and white clothing.

2. *"Those whom I love I rebuke and discipline. So be earnest, and repent."* As a loving Lord, Christ rebukes and disciplines Christians who stray from following Him through life. When we get off His path, we get in spiritually dangerous areas for believers. Christ wants to protect us, so we are disciplined just as children are whose father dearly loves them. The Laodiceans have sinned and not acknowledged it, so Christ calls on them to earnestly repent of their sins of indifference and self-centeredness. They thought they were good Christians—Christ makes it clear that they were sinning and needed to acknowledge it and repent of it. Their apostasy was sickening to Christ, and they were headed for His judgment if those who were spiritually lost didn't repent and accept Him as Savior or if backsliders didn't repent.

3. *"Here I am! I stand at the door and knock. If anyone hears my voice and opens the door, I will come in and eat with him, and he with me."* This Scripture is quoted out of context more than just about any other Scripture in the Bible. It is often quoted as a blanket invitation to unbelievers to accept Christ as their Savior. However, the actual meaning of this passage of Scripture from

Christ is an invitation to the self-deluded professing Christians in Laodicea. The members of this church are invited to listen to Christ's knocking on their church door. Christ has been kept outside of this church by the unconfessed sins of its members, but He wants to come inside and has been knocking on their door for a long period. For them to respond to His knock, the sinning members of the church need to open the door to Him by repenting of their sins and then let Him enter on His own terms, not theirs. He wants to fellowship with them as those who are surrendered to His lordship. We need to observe that Christ will not knock forever at this church's door. If His knock is not responded to by faith, then they can expect to be ejected by premature deaths.

Part III: How Jesus' Encouraged Overcomers of the Church at Laodicea

1.   *"To him who overcomes, I will give the right to sit with me on my throne, just as I overcame and sat down with my Father on his throne."* Overcomers in the Laodicean church are those who repented of and confessed their sins. Christ overcame every flaming arrow of temptation satan shot at Him, and became our Savior and Lord. Overcomers over indifference sins are given the right to sit in a throne ("I saw thrones on which were seated those who had been given authority to judge" [Rev. 20:4]). They are thus given the right of being judges in the Messianic Kingdom.

Christ has **nothing good** to say about any of the Christians in Laodicea. They are sinners who are spiritually blind, and their Great Physician offers to sell them some spiritual eye salve so they will see their peril if they do not repent of their sins.

However, those who overcome either being spiritually lost or guilty of backslidden apostasy by acknowledging and repenting of their sins (and, for the lost, having saving faith in Christ) have a very good outcome in heaven.

Those who do not overcome face unexpected premature death, and any unsaved apostates face a Christless eternity.

Reread Revelation 3:14–22 at the beginning of this chapter. Now take a brief period to answer the following four questions about the Laodicea Church. Finally, answer the fifth question about your local church. Check Y for yes, N for no, CD for cannot determine, and DK for do not know. (Check the answers under this exercise only after you have answered each question as best you can.)

1-Does the worship of members of this church please Christ?
__Y __N __CD __DK
2-Does the *work* of members of this church please Christ?
__Y __N __CD __DK
3-Does the *witness* of members of this church please Christ?
__Y __N __CD __DK
4-What about the Laodicea Church displeases Christ?

_____

5-Which features of the Laodicea Church are present in your local church?

_____

(Answers: 1-N, 2-N, 3-N, 4-They are lukewarm Christians who are spiritually blind and apostate, 5-Answers will vary.)

Dear members and leaders of the Church in Laodicea, what are your answers to the following three questions?

Does the *worship* of members of your church please Christ?

Does the *work* of members of your church please Christ?

Does the *witness* of members of your church please Christ?

The spiritual leaders of this church would answer all the questions, "Yes!"

The members of this church would give the same answer. How dare that anyone would question that these Christians didn't please Christ!

Jesus' verdict is that, no matter how the members and leaders answer these questions, *"You are lukewarm—neither cold nor hot—I am about to spit you out of my mouth!"* (Rev. 3:16). You church people think of your church much more highly than you ought to and I want you to know that you are all in great peril unless you repent.

Jesus Christ offers to salvage the lukewarm Christians in this church. He wants to snatch them away from premature death and the fires of Hell *("I am about to spit you out of my mouth"* [Rev. 3:16]) and turn them in the right direction.

Jesus Christ invites them to *"Be earnest, and repent. Here I am! I stand at the door and knock. If anyone hears my voice and opens the door, I will come in and eat with him, and he with me"* (Rev. 3:19–20). He invites lukewarm believers to come back to Him in repentance, or if they are unsaved to come to Him with repentance and saving faith. To eat a meal with Christ is to have a close relationship with

Him. The invitation is to personal fellowship for all who open the door to invite Christ inside.

In John Newman's sermon about the church being our best representation of heaven (cited in the "Introduction" of this book), he said that we should not talk about the things of the world in church. Instead, in church, we should praise God, worship God, sing to God, thank God, confess to God, give ourselves up to God, and ask for God's blessing.

However, at churches like Laodicea, they constantly talk about the things of the world. They probably even hear sermons about how God can help them secure a firm financial future for their families and be as wealthy as they have the faith to be.

Do the members of your local church hear a lot about the things of the world each Lord's Day? If so, your church has something in common with the Laodicea Church.

Why Don't People in the Laodicean Church Open the Door?

Jesus Christ knocks at the door of the church at Laodicea.

Why doesn't the pastor open the door to Him?

Maybe the pastor earns $150,000 a year, and he knows that if Christ comes into his church that he will have to take a salary cut. Maybe the pastor has a sweet real-estate deal going with one of the big-money members, and he knows that if Jesus comes into his church that the deal is off. Maybe the pastor has an inflated parsonage deduction for his taxes, and he knows that if Jesus Christ comes into his church that his parsonage deduction inflation will be deflated.

Well, if the pastor will not open the door for Christ, then why don't the elders and the deacons open the door to Him?

Maybe the elders and deacons go to church to make business

deals, and they know that if Christ comes into their church, they will have to start singing and praying rather than planning and scheming. Maybe the elders and deacons like receiving the church's blessing on their rich way of life, and they know that if Jesus comes into their church that their focus on riches will change to a focus on poverty. Maybe the elders and deacons like all the special favors they get from the pastor, and they know that if Jesus Christ comes into their church that the poor and the unsaved will get most of the attention and the rich and the famous will have to go to the back of the line.

Well, if the pastor, the elders, and the deacons will not open the door for Christ, then why don't the members get together and let Him inside?

Maybe the members like going to a church that does not push them to be better Christians, and they know that if Christ comes into their congregation that they will be called to righteous instead of self-centered living. Maybe the members like going to a church with lots of successful people, and they know that if Jesus comes into their congregation that their standards for success will have to change. Maybe the members like going to a church that asks little of them, and they know that if Jesus Christ comes into their congregation that they will be required to become an involved, functioning part of His Body.

Christ Continues to Seek Entry into the Lukewarm Church

Even though no one will open the door, Christ continues to knock. But now He must increase the pressure to let Him in and He issues a warning when He declares,

"I know your deeds, that you are neither cold nor hot. I wish

you were either one or the other! So, because you are luke-
warm — neither hot nor cold — I am about to spit you out
of my mouth . . . you do not realize that you are wretched,
pitiful, poor, blind and naked" (Rev. 3:15–17).

If you get ready to drink from what you expect to be a hot cup of coffee, and end up with a mouthful of a lukewarm coffee-flavored liquid, you wouldn't swallow it, would you? Of course, not— you'd likely spit it out in a sink. Jesus expects His Church to be spiritually hot. When He finds a church that is not, He lets the members know the consequences of their sins for He is lovingly seeking for the backslidden apostates to repent of their sins and for the lost to accept Him as their Savior. He can then help them reform themselves and their church. Should His help be spurned, the lukewarm church members will face spiritual ejection.

Christ cries out to the Laodicean Church leaders: "Repent! Turn away from a lifestyle focused on self and turn toward a lifestyle focused on God's kingdom."

Christ does not want big bank accounts flouting their financial power at His Church. He wants people who have any size of bank accounts to surrender everything they have and own to the Lord Jesus Christ.

Christ does not want His Church to major in having first-class facilities. He wants His Church to major in spreading His Gospel so people will have the best possible facilities in heaven.

Christ does not want His Church to be some kind of civic or social club. He wants members of His Church devoted to build up the faith of one another and to pray and be concerned about and accountable to each other. His Church is to be a vital assembly of the family of God.

Christ invited the church at Laodicea to repent with earnestness, then become spiritually hot. Paul wrote to the church at Rome, instructing members of that church to "offer your bodies as living sacrifices, holy and pleasing to God" (Rom. 12:1). All Christians need to surrender their lives to the lordship of Christ.

Paul's words in Romans 12:1 direct members of churches to stop worrying so much about *financial* sacrifices and start being concerned about *personal* sacrifices. He also calls all church members to stop worrying so much about making the ministers and members happy and start being concerned about *making God happy.*

Paul proclaimed, "This is your spiritual act of worship. Do not conform any longer to the pattern of this world, but be transformed by the renewing of your mind" (Rom. 12:1–2).

How a Lukewarm Church Became Spiritually Hot

Amity Presbyterian Church was not lukewarm like the Laodicea Church was. Amity was not full of spiritually indifferent and self-sufficient leaders and members. Amity was not full of apostate Christians. However, Amity was neither spiritually hot nor cold, so it fit the *generic* description of being lukewarm.

At Amity, we saw a major revamping of standards occur. We saw our church go from visiting church members to solicit financial pledges (a worldly standard) to visiting them to offer a devotional Bible study (a spiritual standard).

God revealed to Amity a new direction that focused our minds on spiritual development for the individual rather than financial security for the church.

The pastors at Amity opened the door to Christ, surrendering the leadership of the church to Him. The pastors preached about "putting God first" and making Christ the core of our lives. They worked on practical Bible studies. They trained the elders in prayer and pastoral care. They followed the leadership of Christ, seeking to be good spiritual leaders of the flock of God.

The elders at Amity opened the door and let Christ come in, surrendering their lay leadership roles to Him. The elders visited the sick and infirm. They delivered Bible studies to the homes of the members. They encouraged each member to grow spiritually. They followed the leadership of Christ, seeking to be good examples to the flock of God.

The members at Amity opened the door and let Christ come in, surrendering their lives to His lordship. The members entered each other's homes for food and fellowship. They began to pray for each other. They opened their homes to the elders and participated in a church-wide devotional Bible study program. They followed the leadership of Christ, seeking to be good examples of the family of God and to share their faith with the lost.

The pastors, elders, and members opened the door and let Christ into Amity Presbyterian Church, and He transformed our church from being neither spiritually hot nor cold to spiritually hot.

During the time of reformation at Amity, we sang the first two verses of "Eternal God, Whose Power Upholds" at a Sunday morning worship service. Here are the wonderful words of this hymn that give a message we all need to take into our hearts:

Eternal God, whose power upholds both flower and flaming star,

To whom there is no here nor there, no time, no near nor far,

No alien race, no foreign shore, no child unsought, unknown.

O send us forth, thy prophets true to make all lands thine
own!

O God of love, whose spirit wakes in every human breast;

Whom love, and love alone, can know, in whom all hearts
find rest.

Help us to spread thy gracious reign till greed and hate
shall cease

And kindness dwell in human hearts, and all the earth find
peace!

After I sang these verses, the pastor, whom I stood behind,
told me that it seemed like Christ sang through my lips. Here are
key parts of what the Spirit of Jesus sang that morning:

Christ sang of God's agape (sacrificial) love. *O God of
love, whose spirit wakes in every human breast; whom love, and love
alone, can know, in whom all hearts find rest.* Christ reminded us of
God's eternal agape (sacrificial) love expressed to and through the
lives of His children. He reminded us of God's wonderful loving
presence in the spirit of His children so that they will demonstrate
sacrificial love to others.

Christ sang of His commission to believers. *O send us
forth, thy prophets true to make all lands thine own! Help us to spread
thy gracious reign till greed and hate shall cease and kindness dwell
in human hearts, and all the earth find peace!* Christ reminded us of
our commission from Him that we call the Great Commission (see
Acts 1:8). His followers are to proclaim God's salvation message to
unbelievers and demonstrate wonderful changes in the behavior
of the saved, including expressions of kindness and peace. He

162

reminded us of our duty to witness for Him and rejoice when we see life changes in the newly saved who now fight *against* greed and hate instead of embracing those emotions.

Christ sang of bringing heaven to earth. *Help us to spread thy gracious reign.* Christ called His Church to project God's Kingdom throughout the entire world; in other words: to have heavenly churches all over the world.

Christ sang about removing all prejudices on earth. *Eternal God, to whom there is no alien race, no foreign shore, no child unsought, unknown.* Christ called the members of His church to be color blind and to welcome everyone who is created by Him with open arms of love.

How Does Your Church Compare?

How does your church compare to the one at Laodicea?

Does Christ need to discipline your church with a crisis so that your leaders and members will turn away from the things of the world?

Do not wait too long to ask God to help you change. Delay may lead to Christ spitting your church members out of His mouth. That will mean that those who are false advertisements of the family of God die prematurely and those who are lost experience spiritual death.

A Church That Didn't Want to Become Lukewarm

On the second Sunday of 2005, I stayed home sick and saw Dr. David Hailey of Hayes Barton Baptist Church preach a sermon on television titled "Don't Miss the Point." Dr. Hailey told the congregation that during 2005 they would examine everything they did and that they would make sure that each activity and each program had God as the priority. He warned the congregation that the church may have slipped into some bad habits and that they must realign everything they did with the divine nature of Christ's Church.

In this sermon, Dr. Hailey let Christ into Hayes Barton Baptist Church to insure that they did not become lukewarm like the church at Laodicea. Dr. Hailey wanted his local church to be a heavenly church, on fire for the Lord.

What about *your* local church?

If you suspect that your church has become lukewarm, then act now and invite Christ to come to your church and wake up your congregation and its leaders.

If you think your church is just fine, then think again. In his study of this letter to the church at Laodicea, the biblical scholar William Barclay contended that neutrality and indifference could defeat the cause of Christ at any church. Barclay insisted that each church needed to constantly maintain an examining and questioning mode. That's exactly what Dr. Hailey and the congregation at Hayes Barton Baptist Church did.

Barclay noted that, according to God's Word, out of this intentional cycle of controversy and change, Christ would emerge as the Victor ("Laodicea: Neither One Thing Nor Another," *The New Daily Study Bible: The Revelation of John,* Vol. I).

In Christ's victory, we will open the door of our church and find that Jesus has joined us for dinner. In Christ's victory, we will find the members of our church lifted up to heaven where we will be seated in one of those wonderful heavenly seats beside our Lord Jesus Christ.

"He who has an ear, let him hear what the Spirit says to the churches" (Rev. 3:22).

Christ's Church needs to become spiritually hot!

Suggestions for the Local Church

Rev. Fred C. Holder, the pastor of Amity Presbyterian Church, wrote: "After more than thirty years in the ministry, I have heard over and over again that keeping members active and involved in church life is a perennial problem. Throughout my career, I have heard ministers struggling for ways to assimilate members into the church and help them to grow mentally, emotionally and spiritually—especially spiritually.

Rev. Holder's Information About the AIM Program

I myself have tinkered with different vehicles to accomplish spiritual growth among the members; sometimes I've had a small measure of success, but most of the time I've come up short.

Then came AIM (An Involved Membership), developed by one of the lay leaders at Amity, John Meacham. Here's what AIM will do for a church:

1. The official leadership of the church learns how to minister to the congregation.
2. The official leadership of the church and the pastor(s) become a working team.
3. Pastors learn an effective way to minister to their church members.
4. The members of the church learn how to minister to each other.

Here's what AIM is all about:

AIM (An Involved Membership)

In Romans 14:19, Paul instructs the church that "we must

always aim at those things that bring peace and that help strengthen one another." (*Good News Bible*) God blessed Amity Presbyterian Church with a means to strive toward these ends. The means came in the form of AIM, a five-year program designed to enhance spiritual growth and strengthen the bonds among church members. AIM functions through lay-led, Christ-centered small groups that include all church members. The lay leader-shepherd encourages the group members to become involved in individual spiritual-growth activities, AIM Group fellowship activities, and church-wide functions. This encouragement is accomplished through telephone calls, visits, cards, letters, church publications, weekly bulletins, church announcements, and other methods.

Each year of the AIM program centers on a Bible passage with specific spiritual-growth and human-relationship objectives as follows:

Year 1: Romans 12:1–21—Put God First—Know Each Other

Year 2: John 3:1–21—Be Born In Christ—Understand Each Other

Year 3: John 6:35–58—Grow In Christ—Care for Each Other

Year 4: Matthew 6:1–21—Live In Christ—Love Each Other

Year 5: John 14:1–21—Conquer In Christ—Reach Out to Others

After hearing about the AIM program, many ministers have

asked me: "How do you get church leaders to accept these responsibilities?" I replied that it takes a lot of patience, but your patience will be rewarded. At this writing, we are in our fourth year of AIM at Amity. The program did not enjoy 100% acceptance at first. Some of our elders initially thought ministry was the pastor's job alone and that they should not have to do this type of shepherding program. Others claimed that it wasn't part of their job description as elders.

However, our elders at Amity encouraged each other to be involved in the AIM program. Each elder of our church received group training in the program, and those who needed more than this received individual instruction from a pastor. Though some elders felt the program was outside their job description, they were reminded of their duties from the Presbyterian Church Book of Order: "the elders are responsible for care and nurture of the congregation." What better way for elders to take care of and nurture members of the congregation than through the AIM program?!

Initially, some elders were apprehensive about ministering to the people in their AIM small-groups. However, as the jittery ones brought their concerns to others in their small-groups, intercessory prayers helped change jitters to assurances. Eventually, each elder effectively ministered to a small group that consisted of ten to twelve families. By our second year, we appealed to all of our members to become involved in the AIM small groups. Additional AIM small-group ministries were launched each year. Currently, in Year Four, we have almost 100% of our congregation participating in the AIM program.

Our lay-leaders' persistence and dedication has had a powerful impact upon our congregation. For one thing, the members of our church can no longer say that the church doesn't care for them or that they never hear from the church leaders. Occasionally a group leader will miss contacting a member but, on the average, each member annually receives at least one home visit, two invitations to the eleven o'clock worship service, and three invitations to group fellowship activities. At times, such as on AIM Sundays, I can feel the members' excitement at the morning worship service. For these many reasons, I cannot imagine Amity without AIM. In today's fast-paced world, a church needs lay people ministering to each other in order to survive and flourish.

The contribution and function of lay people cannot be overemphasized in the AIM program. A small group of lay-leaders on the supervising and monitoring Steering Committee at Amity kept on planning for future AIM ministry, soliciting support for the program, showing a willingness to look at new ideas, and listening to constructive criticism. They took their tasks seriously and have maintained and even improved the program.

These lay-leaders showed persistence, vision, and tenacity. I count it a privilege to give my profound gratitude to them for blessing our church and my life. I am thankful to be involved in the AIM program and to have the opportunity to offer this blessing to your congregation.

For more information on this Shepherd Group Program, see the AIM Appendix of this book or e-mail John Meacham, the developer of this program, at john@dazzlinglight.org.

Small-Group Ministries

Many Christian publishers publish curricula for small-group ministries in churches. Coast Publishing Inc, of Castlerock, Colorado, has begun publishing a dynamic small-group Bible study that will eventually involve every book of the Bible. A former pastor who founded a church that is now almost a mega-church in San Diego, Gene French, is the author of the *Striking It Rich* series.

He also led small-groups for several years and developed a small-group series that presents a Bible lesson each week, packaged in a way that will appeal to any adult who attends. Here are the seven-part features of each small-group meeting:

- **Step One: PRAYER**
  Every lesson must begin with your request to God for the Holy Spirit to open your spiritual eyes and speak to your heart.

- **Step Two: READ!**
  Each person reads five to twenty verses (occasionally more), the Bible portion for that week. The principle here is quality, not quantity. We would rather have you read ten verses a week and know what you have read than read five chapters and comprehend nothing.

- **Step Three: THINK!**
  You will be asked to answer one or two questions on each verse you have read. Though simple, the questions will train you to think about what the verses say.

- **Step Four: STUDY!**
  A short commentary, called Treasure Hunt, will follow your reading and provide brief answers to the questions on the assigned verses. This commentary will give you an opportunity to put the verses in perspective and to help you focus on their context, meaning, and practical application to your life today.

- **Step Five: TALK!**
  You need to be prepared to participate in the weekly meeting, using several key small-group discussion

questions from the verses you've read and studied.

- **Step Six: MEMORIZE!**
  During each study, you will be challenged to commit a key verse to your memory. Each verse you memorize will enrich your daily walk with the Lord.

- **Step Seven: APPLICATION!**
  You will be challenged to discuss how you might apply to your life what you have learned from each Bible lesson.

At the present time, Ephesians—Book One (nine lessons), has been published and is available at coastpublishing.com. Later in 2007, Ephesians—Book Two (nine lessons) will be available from this website for small-group study and still later, James—Books One (six lessons) and Two (eight lessons) will be available. Other New Testament books of the Bible will be published in future years. Discounts are offered for group sales to churches and other Christian organizations. The co-writer for the book you hold is also the consulting editor for Coast Publishing's *Striking It Rich* series of books.[1]

Christ's churches can become spiritually hot through programs like AIM and Striking It Rich!

8

Is Your Church Heavenly?

SUMMARY OF ALL SEVEN CHURCHES

1-Orthodox Ephesus Church

Ephesus was the church full of members and leaders who all lost their first love for Christ! Their orthodox Christian lives lacked enthusiasm for a closer walk with Christ. "Orthodox works," that were noticeable in Ephesus, were the fruits of *duty to* Christ instead of *love for* Him.

How to Find Your Lost First Love for Christ

1. *"Remember the height from which you have fallen!"* **(Rev. 2:5a).** Christ told the members and leaders of the church at Ephesus that, no matter how orthodox they were in services to the Lord, they needed to measure how far they had fallen from their initial first love for Christ.

2. After remembering how far you have fallen from your first love for Christ, you realize your need to *"Repent"* **(Rev. 2:5b).** Christ told the church at Ephesus that they needed to repent of their sin of serving him out of obligation and duty (including the sin of letting their

old natures control them to demonstrate orthodox
Christian deeds).

3. After repenting of the sin of yielding to the old nature,
it is time to *"do the things you did at first"* (**Rev.
2:5c**)—surrender to the lordship of Jesus Christ and
thus return to the motivation of your great love for Him
in all that you do to serve Him. This is the third (final)
step back to the first love you had for Christ. Once you
take this step, you find your first love again.

**Members of a heavenly church are surrendered to the
lordship of Jesus Christ.**

2-Rich Smyrna Church

Christ's only direct comment about the behavior of the Smyrna
believers was positive, and we can infer from His counsel a second
praiseworthy statement (their faithfulness to the Lord under
oppression). He evaluated them as being spiritually rich believers
and encouraged them to stand up for Him as they faced enemies of
their faith—even at the cost of their lives.

How to recognize churches like the one in Smyrna: (1) All of
these churches are true to the Word of God; (2) They are dynamic in
consecration, worship, service, and witness; and (3) Their members
grow spiritually each day and are willing to suffer for the cause of
Christ, no matter the consequences.

**Members of a heavenly church each experience
a rich spiritual life.**

3-True and False Pergamum Church

Christ said two positive things about the church at Pergamum: *"I know where you live--where Satan has his throne. Yet you remain true to my name. You did not renounce your faith in me."* They were Christians (1) who took a stand for Christ and (2) did so even under the worst persecution imaginable.

However, Christ was against the Pergamum Church, too: *"You have people there who hold to the teaching of Balaam, who taught Balak to entice the Israelites to sin by eating food sacrificed to idols and by committing sexual immorality. Likewise you also have those who hold to the teaching of the Nicolaitans."* Some of their members had fallen away from Him and held the teachings of Balaam and the Nicolaitans: that immorality and idolatry were okay for Christians because of their spiritual liberty. Those who held false doctrine infiltrated the church's membership and sought to draw away other members.

Christ commanded this church: *"Repent therefore!"* (Rev. 2:16). If the members and leaders could purge themselves of false teaching and repent of their sin, then Christ would reward them in heaven.

Members of a heavenly church are vigilant in fighting against false teaching.

4-Tolerant Thyatira Church

Although Jesus had described six instances of commendable Christian conduct to describe the Christians in the Thyatira Church in one verse of Revelation 2, He devoted *four verses* to the two negative things He had to say about this church: toleration of

173

two areas of false teachings in the church: (1) sexual immorality and (2) idolatry.

Christ informed godly members of the church that He would add no further burden to them (in order to take a stand for Christ in this immoral, idolatrous church was a burden for devoted Christians). These believers sought from within to influence their church that had strayed theologically and biblically.

Members of a heavenly church never tolerate sexual sin and idolatry.

5- Dead Sardis Church

Christ's letter to Sardis was one of the most critical communications of the seven letters He wrote. It was almost all negative, and only mentioned a few in the church who avoided being among the spiritually dead! He targeted most of the members and spiritual leaders of this church for being among the spiritually dead.

He gave five staccato commands to bring correction: *"WAKE UP! STRENGTHEN what remains and is about to die, for I have not found your deeds complete in the sight of my God. REMEMBER, therefore, what you have received and heard; OBEY IT, and REPENT [repent of your sins of playing church and hiding sins]"* (Rev. 3:2–3).

Members of a heavenly church always demonstrate a living faith.

6-Faithful Philadelphia Church

Christ said *nothing* negative about those in the Philadelphia Church! His only direct comments about the behavior of the Philadelphia believers were positive. He evaluated them as being faithful believers who stood up for Him as they faced Jewish and pagan enemies of their faith.

The "door" that Christ opened for the Philadelphia Church and that no one can close is the door of opportunity to preach the gospel. Christ challenges His followers to invite other people to His great home, because He has opened the door to heaven.

Members of a heavenly church eagerly reach the lost for Christ.

7- Lukewarm Laodicea Church

Christ had nothing good to say about any of the Christians in Laodicea, who were lukewarm Christians. They were sinners who were spiritually blind, and their Great Physician offered to sell them some spiritual eye salve so they will see their peril if they do not repent of their sins.

However, those who overcome either being spiritually lost or guilty of backslidden apostasy by acknowledging and repenting of their sins (and, for the lost, having saving faith in Christ) have a very good outcome in heaven.

Members of a heavenly church are spiritually hot!

Members of a heavenly church are:

1. Surrendered to the lordship of Jesus Christ.
2. Hungering for a rich spiritual life.
3. Vigilant in fighting against false teaching.
4. Intolerant of sexual sins and idolatry.
5. Always demonstrating a living faith.
6. Eagerly reaching the lost for Christ.
7. Spiritually hot.

Heavenly Hickory Church

Dr. Fred Stair rested in his den after a strenuous Sunday morning of teaching and preaching at First Presbyterian Church in Hickory, North Carolina, when my mother and I entered the room.

I pointed at Dr. Stair and said, "Look, Mama, there's Jesus."

Dr. Fred Stair was Jesus Christ to me when I was a boy.

Dr. Fred Stair, many years later, sat in his office at the Presbyterian Foundation waiting to see me when I needed help learning how to live with a divine revelation.

When I entered the room, Dr. Stair said, "I can see the Holy Spirit in you today."

Dr. Fred Stair was Jesus Christ to me when I was a young man.

Pastors—Are you Jesus Christ to your congregation?

The People of a heavenly church

Members of a heavenly church need pastors who reflect Jesus Christ to their congregation, who put God first in their lives and in the lives of their congregation, and who proclaim God's Word to the family of God.

At an elders' retreat for our church, when asked what song he would like the group to sing, our richest, most influential leader said, "*The Old Rugged Cross.*" When Jesus was crucified on the cross, He shed His blood to pay the cost of the penalty of sin for all people. A heavenly church is full of church leaders who have accepted Christ as their Savior and Lord, who are saved by the blood of the crucified One.

Pastors and Elders and Deacons—Are each of you Jesus Christ to the world, letting Him live again in and through your committed lives?

Members of a heavenly church need spiritual leaders who reflect Jesus Christ to the world, who will put God first in their lives and in the life of their congregation, and who will convey to the world the message of eternal salvation through Jesus Christ.

A group of young mothers decided to clean up our church's deteriorating nursery. They spent countless hours and dollars painting, fixing toilets, repairing cribs, replacing toys, finding comfortable rocking chairs, and sharing their love. Now, when young families visit our church, the parents often say, "I love your nursery." The sacrifice of time and effort by these young Christian mothers has paid off in making our nursery an appealing area of our church—a factor rated highly by parental visitors to our church in considering making our church theirs.

177

A heavenly church is not a building where we meet other Christians, but it is the assembly of Christians who reach out in love to visitors by providing ministries for every member of their families.

Pastors and Elders and Deacons and Members—Are you Jesus Christ to your church and to your community?

Members of a heavenly church are people who are born again into God's family, who put God first in their lives and in the life of their church family, and whose personal sacrifice reflects the love of Jesus Christ to the world. Such believers have surrendered the controls of their lives to Jesus Christ.

Members of a heavenly church are surrendered to the lordship of Jesus Christ

---

The Altar Call That Was a Taste of Heaven

On the first Lent Sunday for me at a Presbyterian church I served as interim pastor, the elders decided to do something very non-Presbyterian— they requested me to lead in an altar call following the morning worship message.

To begin the altar call in this church, I presented a brief exposition of Romans 12:1–2, then said, "For some of you, this will be the first time you have offered yourself to God as a living sacrifice, because today is your day of salvation. For others, as you again offer yourselves to God as living sacrifices, you are rededicating your lives to the Lord today." I invited everyone who wished to come forward to the foot of the cross at the front of our church (a cross was on a table on the platform) and offer themselves as living sacrifices to God.

I knew that an altar call would probably affect the comfort level of traditionalists in our church. The transition from traditional to contemporary worship format had already affected the comfort level of our traditionalists. It required breaking some old worship habits and learning some new ones. People in the congregation already participated in the interactive worship service I began. Now, for the altar call, they needed to get up out of their seats, and come forward to either receive Christ or rededicate their lives to Christ.

The pianist started playing the favorite gospel song used for invitations in Billy Graham crusades: "Just As I Am." I walked over to the cross and knelt in front of the table holding it. I bowed my head and waited.

A hand fell on my shoulder as someone knelt beside me. Another hand touched my head. Other hands touched me. Many folks kneeled near me. What a joy when members of the congregation joined me at the foot of the cross!

As the music ended, the Holy Spirit embraced us all. I closed the service by leading in praying the Lord's Prayer in unison.

During the altar call, those on their knees transacted heavenly business.

Hearts were breaking. Lives were changing. We were one in the Spirit. We were one in the Lord.

This was a memorable church experience. This was a taste of heaven in church.

Members of a heavenly church hunger for a rich spiritual life.

Just as bank workers are not trained to recognize counterfeit bills, but instead to focus on learning everything about genuine currency, so Christians do not need to study counterfeit religions but must learn everything they can about Christianity. Thus, any deviation from the genuine will be recognized as counterfeit.

Members of a heavenly church are vigilant in fighting against false teaching.

The sexual crimes and sins of many Catholic priests and even some Protestant pastors have caused many in Christ's Church to suffer greatly. In the church of the co-writer of this book, two members of the pastoral staff had to be fired for immoral conduct. Sexual predators prey on children in church and Sunday school settings, so children's ministries have to safeguard their children by requiring prospective workers to submit fingerprints to check against sexual offender databases. Leaders wear distinctive name tags so those without them cannot attend classes where children assemble. Parents need to install porn website-blocking software on computers their children and teens use and make sure computers with access to the internet are public and not private in their homes.

Members of a heavenly church are intolerant of sexual sin and idolatry.

To live by faith is to take a stand for Christ no matter how you are received. It is also to see through the eyes of faith that the Lord Jesus Christ is present everywhere you are present, and His power and strength is available to you. It is to pray, expecting God to answer your prayers, just as a child of a king would expect his father, the king, to respond to his or her needs.

Members of a heavenly church always demonstrate a living faith.

People in the world consist either of the saved or the lost. If we knew where fresh water was available and kept this news from a thirsty person who had run out of water in his desert wandering, it would be a crime. If we know where fresh living water is available and keep this news from those who are spiritually thirsty, it is a sin. Christians know the Source of living water and can lead the lost to the One who wants to save them from the penalty of all their sins.

At our elders' retreat, when asked what goal we needed to establish for the coming year, our richest, most influential leader said, "Tell the people in the neighborhoods surrounding our church about Jesus Christ." No goal for Christians can ever be more important than evangelism. We are either sinners who have found the Savior or we are sinners who are lost in the world. A heavenly church is composed of sinners who have found the Savior and who cannot wait to lead lost sinners to Him.

Members of a heavenly church eagerly reach the lost for Christ

"Therefore, I urge you, brothers, in view of God's mercy, to offer your bodies as living sacrifices, holy and pleasing to God — this is your spiritual act of worship. Do not conform any longer to the pattern of this world, but be transformed by the renewing of your mind. Then you will be able to test and approve what God's will is — his good, pleasing and perfect will" (Rom. 12:1–2).

Members of a heavenly church are spiritually hot.

"In my Father's house are many rooms; if it were not so, I would have told you. I am going there to prepare a place for you" (John 14:2).

A heavenly church consists of people who are heading to heaven, who want sinners to join them there, and who will gladly show them the only path there.

At St. Mary's Church in Oxford University, John Henry Newman preached, "Heaven then is not like this world: I will say what it is much more like—*a church*. For in a place of public worship no language of this world is heard; there are no schemes brought forward for temporal objects, great or small; no information how to strengthen our worldly interests, extend our influence, or establish our credit. These things indeed may be right in their way, so that we do not set our hearts upon them; still (I repeat), it is certain that we hear nothing of them in church. Here we hear solely and entirely of God. We praise Him, worship Him, sing to Him, thank Him, confess to Him, give ourselves up to Him, and ask His blessing. And therefore, **a church is like heaven**; viz. because both in the one and the other, there is one single sovereign subject—religion—brought before us."[1]

Is Your Church Heavenly?

How about your church? How does it measure up to these heavenly standards? Is your church heavenly? Is Christ calling your congregation to reform?

As you consider the characteristics of your church and the characteristics of the seven churches of Revelation, you have had the opportunity in the first seven chapters of this book to evaluate how your church fits the letters Christ wrote. If the negative characteristics of these letters are true about your church, then you must hear the loud call from Christ to reform your church. Your church pastors, your church leaders, and your church members need to pray that the Holy Spirit will make you right in Christ's eyes and lead you in the reform that Jesus longs to occur at your church. You should also pray that Christ Himself will enlighten your church family and lead you on the path of reformation that will result in your church becoming a heavenly church.

If your church is already a heavenly church, praise God! Now you know from Christ's letters to the seven churches in Asia how your church reflects heaven. For the pastors, leaders, and members of a heavenly church are saved, surrendered to Christ's lordship, able to experience a rich spiritual life, vigilant in fighting against false teaching, intolerant of sexual sins and idolatry, able to demonstrate a living faith, eagerly seeking the lost for Christ, and spiritually hot.

In closing, both Dr. Ackelson and I offer up our fervent prayer that each of you belong on earth to a heavenly church.

AMEN.

Appendix
AIM—An Involved Membership

In Romans 14:19, Paul instructs the church that "we must always aim at those things that bring peace and that help strengthen one another." (*Good News Bible)* God blessed Amity Presbyterian Church with a means to strive towards these ends. The blessing came in the form of AIM, a five-year program designed to enhance spiritual growth and strengthen the bonds among church members. AIM functions through lay-led, Christ-centered small groups that include all church members. The lay leader—Shepherd encourages the group members to become involved in individual spiritual growth activities, AIM Group fellowship activities, and church-wide functions. This encouragement is accomplished through telephone calls, visits, cards, letters, church publications, weekly bulletins, church announcements, and other methods.

Each year of the five-year AIM program centers on a Bible passage with specific spiritual growth and human relationship objectives as follows:

Year 1: Romans 12:1–21—Put God First: Know Each Other
Year 2: John 3:1–21—Born In Christ: Understand Each Other
Year 3: John 6:35–58—Grow In Christ: Care for Each Other
Year 4: Matthew 6:1–21—Live In Christ: Love Each Other
Year 5: John 14:1–21—Conquer In Christ: Reach Out to Others

Jesus founded His Church on Peter—a lay leader, and

spread His ministry through other lay leaders, such as Mary, John, Mary Magdalene, and James. In Acts 6:7, we find these lay people caring for the needs of Christ's followers: "So the Word of God spread. The number of disciples in Jerusalem increased rapidly, and a large number of priests became obedient to the faith."

Thus from the beginning, the Church was founded by laypeople willing to help with one another's spiritual development and pastoral care. The purpose of AIM is to offer this New Testament ministry of enhancing spiritual growth and strengthening the bonds among church members through lay-led shepherd groups.

After being born again at a Moravian meeting at Alders Gate, England, John Wesley traveled through Great Britain preaching and leading hundreds of people to Christ. Then, three years later Wesley retraced his footsteps to check on his converts.

What do you think he found?

He found nothing. No church services. No Bible studies. No Sunday schools. No prayer meetings.

He found no evidence of his earlier evangelism and he proclaimed something that he obeyed from that point on: "May I never again lead my fellow man to Christ unless provision has been made for that person's growing in the Lord."

Wesley then began training lay people to lead local small groups in prayer, Bible study, religious discussion, and mutual help in Christian living. And out of these Christ-centered small groups grew what we know today as the Methodist Church.

What about your church? Could your church use help in the spiritual growth and pastoral care of your congregation?

AIM focuses your congregation's attention on these aspects of church life through the annual spiritual-growth emphasis of putting God first, being born in Christ, growing in Christ, living in Christ, and conquering in Christ. AIM helps your church's pastoral care through the annual human-relationship objectives of getting to know each other, understanding each other, caring for each other, loving each other, and reaching out to others.

Why use AIM?

What makes AIM any different from other curricula for adults? AIM is a unique program that will encourage all who participate in it to grow spiritually.

AIM represents a biblical pilgrimage for your congregation. Once the program is launched, your church members will experience a dimension of spiritual enrichment many Christians seldom reach.

The following outline highlights this five-year pilgrimage:

Year 1: Romans 12:1–21—Put God First

In Year One, the idea is for members to review their faith and priorities. It is a year of decision making when one is called truly to put God first. A living sacrifice is required from each member so God, not self, will be first in their lives. The first year is also the orientation to the AIM program.

Year 2: John 3:1–21—Born In Christ

While it is excellent to believe in God and seek to put God first, it is helpful to know that there is a way for one's faith to grow. People sometimes become discouraged because they have such little faith or make such little progress in their faith. "Born In Christ" is a phrase that helps us know that God is actively moving in our lives as Christians and we can only be aware of this by faith.

It also means that we become one with our brothers and sisters in the faith. It further means that God offers us new possibilities for beginning again and our new nature in Christ can replace our old sinful nature.

Year 3: John 6:35–58—Growing In Christ

A child experiences hunger and cries out. Loving parents give food and the child is nourished and grows. Adults may hunger and thirst and reach out for food and drink. And, sometimes, in the human quest for bread and life, a person chooses bread that neither nourishes nor satisfies. Holding on to temporal and physical things, people perish. To grow spiritually is to partake of Christ, who is the Bread of Life. Christ is Bread and Life and to eat this bread is to live spiritually. Eating Christ's flesh is a mystery. But we do know that we must take in Christ until He becomes a vital part of our lives themselves. Taking Christ into our lives, we proceed to grow after His manner of life and teaching until we do as Paul expresses: "until we grow into the stature of the fullness of Christ" and we become witnesses to Christ who *lives* within us.

Year 4: Matthew 6:1–21—Living In Christ

As one is born and grows in Christ, he or she is called upon to live in Christ. To live in Christ is to walk with Christ and talk with Christ. Christian growth is something genuine and not superficial. One grows spiritually through Bible study, worship, prayer, fasting, and doing things of lasting significance. Jesus taught a new and creative way for people to live in the practice of their faith: to seek the approval of God and not man. This life in Christ is or should be rich in prayer. This year of emphasis could greatly enrich the prayer life of individuals and the congregation.

Year 5: John 14:1–21—Conquer In Christ

God in Christ has called us to a glorious existence and reserved for us a place in heaven. This belief allows people to live in faith and die in confidence. Moreover, Jesus becomes the way to God. For Jesus Christ is the Way, the Truth, and the Life. And as Jesus is the Way to God, we Christians need to be the way to Christ for others by going into the world and spreading His good news of salvation. This is in the spirit of what Paul said: "We are therefore Christ's ambassadors, as though God were making his appeal through us. We implore you on Christ's behalf: Be reconciled to God" (2 Cor. 5:20).

In addition to the biblical emphasis, AIM can help your congregation with fellowship, congregational care, prayer, and evangelism. During the first year, you may want to conduct "get to know each other" activities in the shepherd groups and you may even consider asking people to wear name tags at special worship services or at fellowship dinners. In year two, the Shepherds may want to conduct some "group building" activities to help everyone learn more about each other. The third year may be a good time to start encouraging members to take an active interest in the lives of the other people in their shepherd group. Year four may be a good year to promote prayer groups within your church family. In the fifth year, you should try to identify those people whose faith walk is leading them outside of the church and into your community to spread the message of the gospel.

AIM is not an easy program. AIM touches some basic fears that every layperson seems to have, such as: How can we visit other people in the name of Jesus Christ? How can we pray in peoples' homes and when visiting them in the hospital? How should we respond to members' needs when sickness and death are involved? How can we encourage someone who has not attended church in ten years? How should we minister to and care for their brothers and sisters in Christ?

For these Shepherds, we find inspiration and guidance from Peter, who says, "To the elders among you, I appeal as a fellow elder, a witness of Christ's sufferings and one who also will share in the glory to be revealed: Be shepherds of God's flock that is under your care, serving as overseers—not because you must, but because you are willing, as God wants you to be; not greedy for money, but eager to serve; not lording it over those entrusted to you, but being examples to the flock. And when the Chief Shepherd appears, you will receive the crown of glory that will never fade away." (1 Pet. 5:1–4).

These words from Peter speak to both the "AIM group shepherd" and the pastor. In AIM, the pastor serves as the shepherd to the group leaders and their families. This design provides the pastor the opportunity to spend time with each shepherd and to provide them with encouragement and training.

If you choose to use AIM at your church, you can appoint a "steering committee" to administer the details of dividing the congregation into shepherd groups and preparing an activities calendar for each year. You may want the pastor to be a part of the steering committee. Following is a possible AIM activities calendar for year one:

Month 1: Church approval of AIM and appointment of AIM Steering Committee

Month 2: Steering Committee recruits Shepherds and forms Shepherd Groups

Month 3: Steering Committee and Shepherds decide on annual activities

Month 4: Shepherd Group Orientation Gatherings

Month 5: Shepherd Group Orientation Gatherings

Month 6: Shepherd Group Orientation Gatherings

Month 7: AIM Sunday—Shepherds invite all members to a special Sunday Worship Service and the pastor begins a series of sermons on the year's theme passage of Romans 12:1–21.

Month 8: Pastor prepares a daily Devotional Bible Study of Romans 12:1–21.

Month 9: Shepherds deliver Romans 12:1–21 Devotional Bible Study to group members' homes.

Month 10: Shepherds deliver Romans 12:1–21 Devotional Bible Study to group members' homes.

Month 11: Shepherds deliver Romans 12:1–21 Devotional Bible Study to group members' homes.

Month 12: Shepherds invite group members to a picnic for the entire congregation.

If your church is like most, there are many inactive and disinterested members on your roll. It may be tempting to feel that these people are not worth your effort. However, here, Jesus sets our example when we observe that His ministry focused on people outside the temple doors. He saw everyone as a potential child of God and met him or her wherever they were. For example, we read in Mark that when Jesus came to Simon's home and found his mother-in-law in bed with a high fever, He did not ask her whether she had paid her tithe or whether she had said her prayers. He did not ask her if she believed that He was the Messiah. No. "He went to her, took her hand and helped her up. The fever left her and she began to wait on them" (Mark 1:31).

AIM centers around the individual member and works through a process of strengthening the bonds between group members. The "shepherds" serve as group coordinators and will be responsible for delivering the program to each group member and helping with other needed pastoral care that may arise in their shepherd group. The shepherd becomes an assistant to the pastor in caring for the members and a conduit for the church to each member. In the early years of AIM, the pastor may need to invest an extra amount of time in equipping the shepherds to care for the congregation.

As with pastoral care, encouraging spiritual growth begins with each individual's current perspective of his or her separate and distinct relationship with God. When Jesus encountered the woman at the well, He said to her, "Believe me, woman, a time is coming when you will worship the Father neither on this mountain nor in Jerusalem. You Samaritans worship what you do not know; we worship what we do know, for salvation is from the Jews. Yet a time is coming and has now come when the true worshipers will worship the Father in spirit and truth, for they are the kind of worshipers the Father seeks. God is spirit, and his worshipers must worship in spirit and in truth" (John 4:21–24).

The AIM process enhances spiritual growth and places its emphasis on God and the individual, offering Christ as the key to this ever-growing relationship. The design of the program affords each member the opportunity to seek his or her own unique relationship with God, Christ, and the Holy Spirit.

If you choose to incorporate AIM into the life at your church, we hope and pray that it will help you seek God and offer an enriched Christian life for each member.

For more information, you can contact John Meacham, the developer of the AIM program, at *john@dazzlinglight.org*. A booklet about all the aspects of AIM is available free of charge.

Notes

Introduction

[1] Thornton, John F. & Katharine Washburn. *Tongues of Angels Tongues of Men: A Book of Sermons.* New York: Doubleday, 1999. p 529

1. Orthodox Ephesus Church

[1] Thornton and Washburn, *Tongues of Angels.* p 529

2. Rich Smyrna Church

[1] Hughes, Tim. *Here I Am to Worship.* Ventura, California: Regal Books, 2004. p 32
[2] Hughes, *Here I Am,* p 38
[3] Hughes, *Here I Am,* pp 39–44
[4] Hughes, *Here I Am,* pp 41–42
[5] Hughes, *Here I Am,* p 42
[6] Ruis, David. *The Worship God is Seeking.* Ventura, California: Regal Books, 2005. pp 17–20

3. True and False Pergamum Church

[1] *Paul Little.* **Know What You Believe.** *(Colorado Springs, CO: Cook Communications Ministries, 2003) pp 11-12.*
[2] Little. *Know What.* pp 45–46
[3] Little. *Know What.* pp 58–59
[4] Little. *Know What.* pp 71–72
[5] Little. *Know What.* pp 80–81
[6] Little. *Know What.* p 126

5. Dead Sardis Church

[1] Warren, Rick. *The Purpose-Driven Life.* Grand Rapids, Michigan: Zondervan, 2002. p 9
[2] Warren, *Purpose Driven Life.* p 318

6. Faithful Philadelphia Church

[1] Boshart, Martha. *Heaven: Who's Got the Tickets & How Much Do They Cost?* Uhrichsville, Ohio: Barbour Publishing, Inc, 2001. pp 175–177

7. Lukewarm Laodicea Church

[1] French, Gene. *Striking It Rich.* Castlerock, Colorado: Coast Publishing, 2005.

8. Is Your Church Heavenly?

[1] Thornton and Washburn, *Tongues of Angels.* p 529

Bibliography

American Family Association. *2005. American Family Association: AFA Online.* http://www.afa.net/mission.asp [May 13, 2005].

Barclay, William. *The New Daily Study Bible: The Revelation of John Volume One.* Louisville, Kentucky: Westminster John Knox Press, 2004. First published in 1959.

Boshart, Martha. *Heaven: Who's Got the Tickets & How Much Do They Cost?* Uhrichsville, Ohio: Barbour Publishing, Inc, 2001.

Evangelism Explosion International. 2003. "Why EE?" *Evangelism Explosion International.* http://www.eeinternational.org/whyee/page1.html [April 7, 2005].

French, Gene. *Striking It Rich.* Castlerock, Colorado: Coast Publishing, 2005.

Hughes, Tim. *Here I Am to Worship.* Ventura, California: Regal Books, 2004.

Kennedy, Dr. D. James. "Wartime Living," *Multiply #2/2004.* http://www.eeinternational.org/news/Mult/0604.htm [April 6, 2005].

Little, Paul E. *Know Who You Believe The Magnificent Connection.* Colorado Springs: Cook Communications Ministries, 2003.

Little, Paul E. *Know Why You Believe Connecting Faith and Reason.* Colorado Springs: Cook Communications Ministries, 2003.

Little, Paul E. *Know What You Believe Connecting Faith and Truth.* Colorado Springs: Cook Communications Ministries, 2003.

Ruis, David. *The Worship God is Seeking.* Ventura, California: Regal Books, 2005.

Thornton, John F. & Katharine Washburn. *Tongues of Angels Tongues of Men: A Book of Sermons.* New York: Doubleday, 1999.

Warren, Rick. *The Purpose-Driven Life.* Grand Rapids, Michigan: Zondervan, 2002.

Warren, Rick. *40 Days of Purpose Overview.* http:// www.saddlebackresources.com/en-US/Campaigns/ 40DaysOfPurpose/DOPOverview.htm [February 9, 2008].

Wildmon, Tim. April 2005. "Why Caring About Culture Is No Waste of Time," *AFA Journal.* http://www.afajournal.org/2005/ april/4.05tim.asp [May 13, 2005].

Referenced Websites

American Family Association at www.afa.net

Appalachia Service Project at www.asphome.org

Evangelism Explosion at www.eeinternational.org

40 Days of Purpose at www.purposedriven.com

Striking It Rich at www.coastpublishing.com

The Dazzling Light at www.dazzlinglight.org

Author Biographies

John Meacham, a lay pastor in the Presbyterian Church, has a heart for serving the Lord and others in the body of Christ. Whether John is preaching, teaching, leading small groups, facilitating workshops or writing, his personal relationship with God has been made richer by following his calling.

John resides in Raleigh, North Carolina with Sue, his cherished wife of thirty-four years. Their sons Brian and James are both married, and their granddaughter Emma is a constant delight.

The Meachams are both originally from Hickory, North Carolina. They are graduates of the University of North Carolina at Chapel Hill, and are very active in their church. When their busy schedules allow, they love spending time together in the Blue Ridge Mountains.

Lon Ackelson, Th.D., has been a professional editor/ writer for close to thirty years. While he has numerous credits to his name, his many years of experience as an ordained pastor and his background as a Bible teacher on the graduate and post-graduate level have given him the expertise needed to work with John on writing *Is Your Church Heavenly?*

Lon currently lives in Poway, California with the love of his life, Janet, his wife of thirty-seven years. The Ackelsons, formerly from Arizona, made the move to San Diego when Lon was offered the position of senior editor for Christian Ed Publishers. He later began his own editing company, Lighthouse Editing. The couple remains active in their church where Lon continues to teach Bible classes in the church's Bible Institute, Sunday school, and small group Bible Studies. When Lon finds time to himself, he enjoys reading a good book or solving a crossword puzzle.

To order additional copies of *Is Your Church Heavenly?* or the *Group Study Guide* for *Is Your Church Heavenly?* please visit our website www.zoelifepub.com. On the website you will also find information about other books by John Meacham or Zoë Life Publishing.

A bulk discount is available when 12 or more books are purchased at one time.

Contact Outreach at Zoë Life Publishing:

Zoë Life Publishing
P.O. Box 871066
Canton, MI 48187
(877) 841-3400
outreach@zoelifepub.com